RELATING TO LAW

A Chronology of Women and Law in Canada

SECOND EDITION

edited by

T. BRETTEL DAWSON

Associate Professor, Department of Law
Carleton University, Ottawa

CANADIAN LEGAL STUDIES SERIES

CAPTUS PRESS

Relating To Law:
A Chronology of Women and Law in Canada
Second Edition

This selection Copyright © 1994 by T. Brettel Dawson and Captus Press Inc.

ISBN 1–895712–56–4

The publisher and the editor gratefully acknowledge the authors, publishers and organizations for their permission to reproduce their work in this book. Care has been taken to trace ownership of copyright material contained in this book. The publisher will gladly take any information that will enable it to rectify any reference or credit in subsequent editions and apologizes for any errors or omissions.

Canadian Cataloguing in Publication Data

Main entry under title:

Relating to law: a chronology of women and law
    in Canada

(Canadian legal studies series)
2nd ed.
Includes bibliographical references.
ISBN 1–895712–56–4

1. Women – Legal status, laws, etc. – Canada.
I. Dawson, B. (Brettel).   II. Series.

KE509.Z82R44 1995   349.71'082   C95–930317–0
KF478.Z9R44 1995

10 9 8 7 6 5 4 3 2 1
Printed in Canada

This book is dedicated to mothers in general, and to my mother Irene Harris in particular. Her death in 1993 marked a profound change in my life. I cherish her memory, value her love and support, and miss her dearly.

Table of Contents

Preface

The idea for this project of "remembering" historical markers of particular relevance to women in Canada developed out of a larger undertaking of compiling and editing readings for use in university courses concerned with law and gender. (See T. Brettel Dawson, *Women, Law and Social Change: Core Readings and Current Issues*, 2d ed. Toronto: Captus Press, 1993.) It seemed to be of particular importance that a broader context be sketched in to give a perspective and a consciousness of the past and its interactions with current issues, debates and developments.

Jennifer Quaile has provided extraordinary research assistance in this revision and I offer her my thanks and appreciation. In the original edition of this book, I received excellent research assistance from Seema Kalia, Donna Shiplett and Laura Landry, together with valuable collegial input from Mary Jane Mossman and Susan Boyd which helped to enrich the creative process. The knowledge shared by Adrienne Shadd and Constance Backhouse was of great assistance. Thanks also to M. Angela MacDonald who provided encouragement and sustenance.

Any errors, infelicities or editing flaws remain my responsibility. I welcome comments and suggestions for consideration in subsequent editions.

T. Brettel Dawson
Department of Law
Carleton University
Ottawa, Ontario
November 1994

Introduction

A foreshortened view of history is not uncommon among an undergraduate student body. Events of 10 years ago are regarded as being "really old" presumably because they are at the fringes of individual memory. Similarly, occurrences beyond a 10-year vintage tend to be simply unknown. Such an approach risks the loss of a huge amount of collective experience, relevant for understanding our histories and their legacies, and providing context and nuance to current debates. This volume aims to provide a general (and admittedly idiosyncratic) overview of a broad range of historical and statistical material of particular relevance to women in Canada, with an emphasis on the role of law and legal institutions as sites of regulation, resistance, change, and complexity. My objectives are to provide a lengthened view of women's legal history and to lay the basis for a process of remembering, reflecting, celebration and critique. The importance of knowing our histories is eloquently put by Gerda Lerner, a feminist historian:

> History gives meaning to life, and connects each life to immortality. But history has yet another function; in preserving the collective past and reinterpreting it to the present, human beings define their potential and explore the limits of their possibilities. We learn from the past not only what people before us did and thought and intended; we also learn how they failed and erred.[1]

What we learn from legal history is that the relationship between law(s) and social change is complex. Actions can have both intended and unintended consequences. A range of conflicting interests can interact to motivate and drive initiatives for change. Visions of the "good society" are contested, as are definitions of the existence and nature of social "problems" requiring remedy (and indeed, of the appropriate remedy). While law is undoubtedly a site of power, including the power to define, law can also "provide a forum for articulating alternative visions and accounts."[2] Law does not have one single appearance or form, nor is it of a monolithic or unitary character. Contradiction, disputation, and uneven development characterize the living and social nature of law and legal regulation. Carol Smart has pointed out that law develops unevenly and she has emphasized that this

> rejects completely any concept of law as a unity which simply progresses, regresses, or reappears as a cycle of history to repeat itself... To analyze law [in terms of its uneven development]...creates the possibility of seeing law both as a means of "liberation" and, at the same time, as a means of the reproduction of an oppressive social order. Law both facilitates change and is an obstacle to change....[3]

It is often important to analyze the influences on ideas constructed and expressed within the legal arena, and the ways in which dissenting opinions may eventually inform and even be embraced by the mainstream. At the same time, it is important not to ascribe motives for "progressive" views without the benefit of context. Norma Basch has compellingly demonstrated that the legislative motivations for the enactment of Married Women's Property Acts in the nineteenth century, which permitted married women to own property, were driven by creditors who was anxious to collect debts. Thus, the legislation was not primarily directed to enhancing the legal status of women,[4] although it undoubtedly had that effect over time.

---

[1] Gerda Lerner, *The Creation of Patriarchy* (New York and Oxford: Oxford University Press, 1986) at 221.
[2] Carol Smart, *Feminism and the Power of Law* (London: Routledge, 1989) at 88.
[3] Carol Smart, "Feminism and Law: Some Problems of Analysis and Strategy" (1986) 14 International Journal of Law and Sociology 109 at 117.
[4] See Norma Basch, *In The Eyes of the Law: Women, Marriage and Property in Nineteenth-Century New York* (1982).

With these ideas in mind, this book presents three different sets of material to approach the interwoven matter of the social and legal status of women and efforts to ensure women's integration into the discourses of law and their inclusion (or in some cases, continuing exclusion) in the polity. The first section of the book draws together a range of judicial observations about women and their place(s). These comments were at once the product of a particular band of thinking of the time (which had access to the power of law to define) and a product of the precepts of legal reasoning which favoured current understandings of the role of precedent authority and canons of statutory interpretation. (Nevertheless, it can be noted that in some of these cases, the judges were in flagrant breach of the rules of precedent, method and reasoning which they were allegedly following.) It is a debatable question as to whether the judges were conscious of the biases inherent in their views about the capacity (and appropriateness) of women to undertake societal roles different from those that had been assigned to (at least middle class, white women). It is also instructive to note how abstracted and formalized a view of women is articulated by these judges. Where is the experience of working class women, or aboriginal women or non-White women? What is the significance of their absence? To what extent is there a similar limited construction of women (and men) in legal discourse today? To what extent is there a similar resistance to changes in society (and legal) roles for women (and men) today? What is our current sense of the "natural" and "inevitable," of the *status quo*, does it obscure injustice and exclusion?

The second section of this book presents an annotated chronology of women's legal history, primarily in Canada. The chronology notes women's "firsts" and significant pieces of legislation. It also provides some context for the changes, including contemporary statements and some updates. This section is designed to be browsed, providing a general reference to a range of events. It is by no means exhaustive or comprehensive.

The third section of the book presents a statistical overview of women's status in Canadian society. The material is structured around Canada's Third Report to the United Nations under the Convention for the Elimination of All Forms of Discrimination Against Women (CEDAW). The official views of that document are nuanced, supplemented, challenged and updated in parallel sourcing from the Canadian Advisory Council on the Status of Women and a variety of other sources. This material supplements the historical material by creating a current picture of women in Canada, and providing a basis to evaluate policy initiatives and ongoing areas requiring advocacy and change.

I hope that the material collected in this book will help to situate a reader interested in women's relationships with law and legal processes within a broad spectrum of women roles in Canadian life — from past to present, and including aspects of class, gender, race/ethnicity, sexual orientation and (dis)ability. The material can be used to locate some of the historical sources of legal arguments and concerns, to identify and trace the effects of underlying premises and assumptions in law, and to analyze the relationships between women's legal status and their social, economic and political roles. The process, of course, is one of shaping meanings from events and expressed ideas. As a result, it is important to view these comments, markers and statistics as raw materials for making meanings about women's lives.

Benchmarks: What Judges Have Said about Women over the Years

Judges have an important role in the legal system. They articulate, interpret and apply legal principles to fact situations brought before them by litigants unable to settle their disputes. The "official" version of the judicial function[1] is that judges are to be objective or impartial and to utilizing legal method in reaching decisions.[2] Where judges give written reasons for their disposition of a case, they are referred to as the "decision," "opinion" or "judgement" on the case. Many judgements, particularly at the appeal level, are published in series of case reports and become part of the body of law consulted by judges, lawyers and researchers. In this section, I draw together a range of observations about women which have been included in judges' decisions.

As noted in the Introduction, the statements made by the various judges were at once the product of a particular band of thinking of the time (to which judges are not immune despite the abstraction claimed by the official or positivist version of legal process) and the precepts of legal reasoning which favoured current understandings of the role of precedent authority and canons of statutory interpretation. From today's perspective, these statements show a clear bias against women. But it is a debatable question as to whether the judges were conscious of the biases inherent in their views about the capacity (and appropriateness) of women to undertake societal roles different from those assigned to (at least middle class, white women). What is also notable are a range of recurring themes, appeals to sociobiology, social structures and decorum, and a profound sense that the inclusion of women has been problematic, unsettling and uncertain.

RECURRING THEMES

In 1869, Sophia Jex-Blake and six other women, together known as the "Edinburgh Seven," were rebuffed in their attempt to study at the Edinburgh Medical School. Lord Neaves, a member of the full bench of the Scottish Court of Session which heard the women's appeal in 1873, had little apparent hesitation in supporting the expulsion of the women from the School. In his decision he stated:

It is a belief, widely entertained that there is great difference in the mental constitution of the two sexes, just as there is in their physical conformation. The powers and susceptibilities of women are as noble as those of men; but they are thought to be different, and, in particular, it is considered that they have not the same power of intense labour as men are endowed with. If this be so, it must form serious objection to uniting them under the same course of academic study. I confess that, to some extent, I share this view, and would regret to see our young females subjected to the severe and incessant work which my own observation and experience have taught me to consider as indispensable to any high attainment in learning.

A disregard of such an inequality would be fatal to any scheme of public instruction, for, as it is certain that the general mass of an army cannot move more rapidly than its weakest and slowest portion, so a general course of study must be toned and tempered

---

[1] To further explore ideas about judging, refer to Hon. Bertha Wilson, "Will Women Judges Really Make a Difference?" (1990) 28 Osgoode Hall Law Journal 507. J.A.G. Griffiths, *The Politics of the Judiciary*, 2d ed. (London: Fontana, 1981); Peter Russell, *The Judiciary in Canada: The Third Branch of Government* (Toronto: McGraw-Hill Ryerson, 1987).
[2] See also Mary Jane Mossman, "Feminism and Legal Method: The Difference it Makes" (1897) 3 Wisconsin Women's Law Journal 147, and (1986) 3 Australian Journal of Law and Society 30.

down to suit the average of all the classes of students for whom it is intended; and that average will always be lowered by the existence of any considerable numbers who cannot keep pace with the rest.

Add to this the special acquirements and accomplishments at which women must aim, but from which men may easily remain exempt. Much time must, or ought to be, given by women to the acquisition of a knowledge of household affairs and family duties, as well as to those ornamental parts of education which tend so much to social refinement and domestic happiness, and the study necessary for mastering these must always form a serious distraction from severer pursuits, while there is little doubt that, in public estimation, the want of these feminine arts and attractions in a woman would be ill supplied by such branches of knowledge as a University could bestow.

...[this] case certainly affords no ground from subverting the constitution of our universities, or affecting the dignity and weight which belong to the highest honour attending the medical profession.... Any change which would incur the risk of lowering the standard that now exists, and which we have seen exemplified in so many of our great physicians and professors, is infinitely to be deprecated, and such a danger, I think would be incurred by the revolution in the medical teaching of our universities that has here been attempted to be brought about; while at the same time it would otherwise affect and in my opinion, deteriorate our Universities in a way unknown to any period of their history.[3]

His reasoning, ponderous as it is, contains within it several ideas that are recurring themes in a number of judicial pronouncements. He assumed that "excellence" would be compromised by the admission of women to the universities and the professions. He believed that women are either less intelligent or intellectually less rigorous than men. In his view, women were best suited to a private role confined to domestic pleasures and pursuits. He did not acknowledge that such a separation of private and public spheres provided great benefit to (professional, white,

heterosexual) men who were thereby provided with home comforts, social standing and offspring. Nor did he acknowledge that women were economically marginalized by this arrangement, by being made dependent on male economic capacities. In this way, the "feminization" of poverty has a long history. The judge also assumed that social roles were set. And, were women to work or study outside the home, it was assumed that women would undertake a "double day," not that social or household arrangements would themselves have to change. There is no hint in his reasoning that observable differences in ability and interests between women and men were socially, rather than biologically, constructed and that they had been rigorously enforced and thus perpetuated or "naturalized." Finally, he did not acknowledge that his happy domestic sphere applied only to women of his particular class and race.

Nevertheless, the Edinburgh Seven were expelled from the Medical School.

The idea that a judge's views can mirror the tenor of the times (and that this judge's views did) finds a ready link in the case of Lord Neaves. At about the same time, Herbert Spencer was writing his then leading treatise, *The Principles of Biology*, which explained that sex differences were a product of mankind's successful adaptation to social survival and hence should not be interfered with by law or politics (Spencerian Darwinism). His views, which were very influential on the intellectual climate of the time, indicated:

> That absolute or relative infertility is commonly produced in women by mental labour carried to excess.... This diminution of reproductive power is not shown only by the greater frequency of absolute sterility; nor is it shown only in the earlier cessation of childbearing; but it is also shown in the very frequent inability of such women to suckle their infants.... Most of the flat-chested girls [sic] who survive their high pressure education are incompetent to do this.... It must be contended that no considerable alteration in the careers of women can be, or should be, produced, and further, that any extensive change in the education of women, made with a view of fitting them for business or professions would be mischievous. (1861)[4]

---

[3] *Septem Contra Edinem* (Court of Session, Scotland, 1873), as cited in Albie Sachs and Joan Hoff-Wilson, *The Sexism of Law* (Oxford: Martin Robertson, 1979) at 14–22.

[4] Herbert Spencer, *Principles of Biology*, vol. 2 (London: 1867), at 512–513; *Principles of Sociology* vol. 1 (London, 1876) at 792, as cited in Constance Backhouse, "To Open the Way for Others of My Sex: Clara Brett Martin's Career as Canada's First Women Lawyer" (1985) 1 Can. J. of Women and the Law 1 at 3–4. See also Jane Lewis, "Motherhood Issues in the Late Nineteenth and Twentieth Centuries" in *Delivering Motherhood*, eds. K. Arnup, A. Levesque and R. Roach Pierson (London: Routledge, 1990) at 1.

In 1873, Dr. Edward Clarke, an eminent medical professor of the Harvard Medical School, warned against dire consequences to women from the rigours of education. He warned that women would lose their reproductive capacity if they tried to study beyond puberty. Moreover, "if women were to study they would end up with monstrous brains and puny bodies...weak digestion...and constipated bowels."[5]

This "closed body" rationale was clearly not accepted by all. The words of New Zealander Ethel Benjamin, who on May 11, 1897, became the second woman to be admitted to the practice of law in the British Empire, provided a wry counterpoint to such views. Benjamin had consistently placed a sole — or bracketed — first in her law school examinations. In the course of an interview with Kate Sheppard, published in 1897 in the suffrage magazine *The White Ribbon*, she was asked if she had been adversely affected by her studies. She commented:

> No, my health did not suffer in the least. Do I look like an invalid? I went to bed at 11 o'clock every night and gave myself an allowance of nine or ten hours rest, and, as you can see, this plan has agreed with me pretty well. I believe if students would give themselves a more liberal allowance of resting time they would do better work, and injure their health less. The minimum time in which the LL.B. degree can be taken is four years, and I did it in that time.[6]

Nevertheless, it was not only university education and the practice of medicine by women which were regarded by some as being unsuitable for women and as tempting dire consequences for society. The legal profession, public office, voting and legal personhood itself, were all "off-limits" to women.

BIOLOGY AND DESTINY

An even less generous line of reasoning to the separate spheres theory was that women were intellectually inferior to men. In *Daniels* v. *Clegg* 28 Mich. 32 (1873), a U.S. court, when concerned with the standard of diligence required of a twenty-year-old woman, decided that she should not be required to conform to the standards of the "reasonable man." Rather, concessions were made for her because of "the incompetency indicated by her age and sex — without evidence (of which there is none) of any unusual skill or experience on her part — was less in degree, it is true than in the case of a mere child; but the difference is in degree only, and not in principle."

This approach was also apparent in *The Queen* v. *Crosthwaite* (1867), 17 Irish Common Law Reports 463. The question at issue was, whether a woman was included when the term "persons" was used in the *Towns Improvement (Ireland) Act, 1854*, 17–18 Vict., c. 103 (U.K.). Baron Deasy stated that:

> [T]he general policy of the law is to exclude [women] from any such intervention...partly on the supposition that such subjects are beyond their cognizance, as requiring a judgment superior to that which they possess, and partly on the ground that it is inconsistent with the delicacy and modesty of their sex, that they should be mixed up in the strife and turmoil of a contested election. (at 472)

> ...That the law in recognizing the distinction of the sexes assumes a greater worthiness in the male than in the female, is manifest in the law of descent; that it has regard to the infirmity of bodily strength and ability in the female, by rendering her incompetent for some offices and privileges, or incapacitating her from the discharge of duties thereto belonging, cannot be questioned. Again, that she is subject to incapacities from a presumed inferiority of discretion and judgment, seems also certain: a woman was not admitted as a witness in a case of villeinage [sic] against a man; and the reason assigned is, because of her "fragility." (at 475)

In the same case, Baron Fitzgerald wholeheartedly agreed with his judicial brother and added for himself that he could:

> have no doubt that in substance the reason of the Common Law still applies; and that the course of education and mental training to which women, happily for us and themselves, are subject, does render them far less fit than men for the administration of public affairs.... Having regard to every one of the reasons of Common Law, the subordination of sex, the inferiority of bodily ability, and the mental inferiority in the sense explained...I am not sorry...to come to the conclusion that this judgment ought to be reversed. (at 479)

---

[5] Edward H. Clarke, M.D., *Sex in Education or a Fair Chance for the Girls* (Boston, 1873 [reprinted New York, 1972]), cited in Barbara Ehrenreich and Deirdre English, *For Her Own Good: 150 Years of the Expert's Advice to Women* (Garden City, NY, 1989), at 125–131.
[6] Cited in Carol Brown, Ethel Benjamin: New Zealand's First Woman Lawyer (B.A. Honours Thesis, Department of History, Otago University, N.Z., 1985) [unpublished].

The separate spheres doctrine was linked to biology and intermeshed with natural and divine law by Justice Bradley in a concurring opinion in the case of *Bradwell* v. *Illinois* 83 U.S. (16 Wall) 130 (1879). In this case, Myra Bradwell, who had legal education and had published a successful legal newspaper in Chicago, was petitioning the court for permission to become a practising lawyer. She based her case on the U.S. Constitution which provided that no state should make laws abridging the "rights or immunities of citizens," which Bradwell took to include the economic right to practice a profession. Her case went all the way to the U.S. Supreme Court, where her petition was dismissed. Interestingly, 60 of the leading lawyers of Chicago petitioned the state governor to appoint her as a Notary Public while her case was pending in the Supreme Court. And, three years after the decision, Bradwell did become an honorary member of the bar.[7] However, in court, the judges gave the matter short shrift. In the words of Bradley J.:

> Civil law as well as nature herself has always recognized a wide difference in the respective spheres and destinies of man and woman. Man is, or should be, woman's protector and defender. The natural and proper timidity and delicacy which belongs to the female sex evidently unfits it for many of the occupations of civil life. The constitution of the family organization, which is founded in the divine ordinance, as well as in the nature of things, indicates the domestic sphere as that which properly belongs to the domain and functions of womanhood. (at 141–42)

BIOLOGY, DESTINY AND THE SPHERES OF SOCIAL LIFE

Clearly to Justice Bradley, there were "separate spheres" which dictated that women's role was properly restricted to domesticity and reproduction. Again, the judge was not alone in publicly stating such views.

The medical literature so thoroughly and engagingly surveyed by Christine Ball,[8] supplies some interesting examples, including the views of one John Dalton:

> the female naturally having the immediate care of the young after birth and the male being occupied in providing food and protection for both, there are also corresponding differences in the general structure of the body, which affect the whole external appearance of the two sexes, which even show themselves in their mental and moral, as well as in their physical characteristics.[9]

The "draining effect" of menstruation and other physical attributes of women indicated to a Dr. A.W. Chase, that "the wise use of female energy ruled out overwork, higher education, excitable reading and other strains on the female constitution."[10] Sexual activity not directed to reproductive purposes was referred to as "fraudulent," and some of these practices, such as masturbation and "intense venereal orgasms," purportedly exhausted wives.[11] Nevertheless, housewifery was considered to have beneficial effects. Thus "every young wife, let her station be ever so exalted, ought to attend to her household duties. Her health, and consequently her happiness, demand the exertion. The want of occupation — healthy, useful occupation — is a fruitful source of discontent, of sin, of disease, and barrenness."[12] Another medical commentator opined that "the active period of a woman's life is spent in germinating and suckling her offspring, during which time she is physically capable of little else."[13]

Yet these medical experts — like the judges — appear to have had a limited appreciation of the nature of women's lives and work within the home at that time. (Or, of the fact that a very large number of women worked outside the home or that African-American women, bore the economic and social legacies of slavery and Aboriginal women bore the legacies of colonization.) An evocative description of such work is contained in a letter of support written

---

[7] See generally, Martha Minow, "Forming Under Everything That Grows" [1985] Wisconsin Law Review 819 at 846–50.

[8] Cited in Christine Ball, "Female Sexual Ideologies in Mid to Late Nineteenth-Century Canada" (1986) 1 Can. J. Women and the Law 324 at 331. Ball also cites medical articles concerned with the effect of sewing machines on menstruation, and the effect of menstruation on the curing of meat. Women's reproductive capacities were also regarded by some medical authors of the time as not only leading to physical instability in women but also "to the direct thwarting of instinctive and moral feelings." W.H. Smith, *Smith's Family Physician* (1869) at 15.

[9] John Dalton, *Treatise on Human Physiology Designed for Use of Students and Practitioners of Medicine* (1861) at 526.

[10] A.W. Chase, *Dr. Chase's Recipes: or Information for Everybody; an invaluable collection of about eight hundred practical recipes for merchants, grocers, saloon-keepers, physicians, druggists, tanners, shoemakers, harness makers, painters, jewellers, blacksmiths, tinners, gunsmiths, farriers, barbers, bakers, dyers, renovators, farmers, and families generally* (London, Ontario: E.A. Taylor, 1867) at 210.

[11] See Ball, at 332, citing Louis Bergeret, *The Preventive Obstacle; or Conjugal Onanism* (New York: Arno Press, 1974 [1870]) at 123–25.

[12] Henry Chavisse Pye, *Advice to a Wife and Advice to a Mother on the Management of her Own Health* (1861) at 71.

[13] Hughes Bennett, "Reflections on the Higher Education of Women from a Medical Point of View, Suggested by the Health of Pupil Teachers" (1879) 3:10 The Sanitary Journal 399, at 399.

in 1923 to Dr. Marie Stopes, an advocate of accessible and legal birth control for women:

> In sincerity I write to wish you the best of luck in your Action.... To the men who condemn you, I would like to give one month as a mother in a working man's home. Four bedrooms and scullery with whitewashed walls, stairs devoid of carpet in an obscure corner. The kitchen, which serves as dining room, bakehouse and bedroom when the mother is ill, can boast of papered walls and gas light. The men who condemn you would have to run this house. The weekly wage would be £3 (that is more than average), have two babies one and a half years and three years and prepare for the third.... They would have to feed the family, wash for it, bake for it, clean for it, make a big dinner for one and a half pence each, make old clothes into new. This would be fairly hard but "God Help Them!" what would they do if they were handicapped by pregnancy. You wouldn't have one enemy, they would all commit suicide. Yours truly, an admirer.[14]

PROPRIETY:
PROFESSIONS AND THE VOTE

Annie MacDonald Langstaff, a resident of Quebec, petitioned the Quebec Superior Court in 1915, after her application to take the preliminary bar examination was refused because she was a woman. Her petition was rejected and she was met with this response by Mr. Justice Saint-Pierre:

> I would put within the range of possibilities though by no means a commendable one, the admission of a woman to the profession of solicitor or to that of *avoué*, but I hold that to admit a woman and more particularly, a married woman as a barrister, that is to say, as a person *who pleads cases at the bar before judges or juries in open court and in the presence of the public*, would be nothing short of a direct infringement upon public order and a manifest violation of the law of good morals and public decency.
>
> Let us for a moment picture to ourselves a woman appearing as defending or prosecuting counsel in a case of rapt (sic) [rape] and putting to the complainant the questions which must of all necessity be asked in order

to make proof of the acts which are of the essence of the crime or which are equally necessary to meet and repeal the charge.

> No woman possessing the least sense of decency could possibly do so without throwing a blur upon her own dignity and without bringing into utter contempt the honour and respect due to her sex. (emphasis in original)[15]

A mixture of subtly ridiculing women, while basing a decision on language of decency, respect and honour was another approach to resisting changes in women's position. This "pedestal" approach had been used by the English courts when rejecting the electoral registrations of women in Manchester, England, in 1867. More than 5,000 women had sought to have their names entered on the register of local voters. The governing legislation permitted "men" to be registered. Some women were successful in having their names added to the voters rolls, only to have them taken off again by the revisers. Their objections to this removal resulted in a series of legal cases. In one of these, *Chorlton* v. *Lings* (1868), L.R. 4 C.P. 374, Sir James Easte Willes rationalized the refusal to permit women to vote in the following terms:

> What was the cause of the exclusion of women, it is not necessary to go into: but admitting that fickleness of judgment and liability to influence have sometimes been suggested as the ground of exclusion, I must protest against it being supposed to arise in this country from any under-rating of the sex either in point of intellect or worth. That would be quite inconsistent with one of the glories of our civilization — the respect and honour in which women are held. This is not a mere fancy of my own but will be found in Seldon, in the discussion of the origin of the exclusion of women from judicial and like public functions, where the author gives preference for this reason, that the exemption was founded upon motives of decorum, and was a privilege of the sex. (at 380)

Mr. Justice Byles, in the same case, considered the interpretation to be given to the term "man" in the legislation and stated:

> No doubt, the word "man" in a scientific treatise on zoology or fossil organic remains, would include men, women and children, as constituting the highest order of vertebrate

---

[14] Cited in Shelley Gavigan, "On Bringing on the Menses: The Criminal Liability of Women and the Therapeutic Exception in Canadian Abortion Law" (1986) 1 Can. J of Women and the Law 279 note 155, at 302.
[15] *Dame Langstaff v. The Bar of the Province of Quebec* (1915), 47 Q.S.C. 131 at 139–40.

animals. It is also used in an abstract and general sense in philosophical or religious disquisitions. But, in almost every other connection, the word "man" is used in contradistinction to "woman." Certainly this restricted sense is its ordinary and popular sense. (at 392)

Clearly, judges were proving to be obdurate. Applications by women for admission to the legal profession, for example, are littered with protestations of judicial indignation. Mabel French, who became the first woman to be admitted to the practice of law in New Brunswick in 1906, had met with this response from Mr. Justice Tuck: "If I dare express my own views, I would say that I have no sympathy with the opinion that women should in all branches of life come in competition with men. Better let them attend to their own legitimate business."[16] Frequently, statutory change was needed to open the way for women to enter the professions and to bring into play the influence of individual legislators, social movements and political processes.

LEGAL INVOCATIONS AND OTHER MAGIC

The antipathy of the English judges to the exercise by women of public offices was ideologically entrenched. The legal soundness of their positions, from the point of view of adherence to internal legal method (the official version, anyway), was less secure. In cases such as *Beresford-Hope* v. *Lady Sandhurst*, 23 Q.B.D. 79, and *DeSouza* v. *Cobden*, [1891] 1 Q.B. 687, the legally questionable proposition that women were "not, in general, deemed capable of exercising public functions" was advanced as axiom. In *Beresford-Hope*, the Master of the Rolls, Lord Esher, (the president of the English Court of Appeal) asserted that he took it that "by neither the common law nor the constitution of this country from the beginning of the common law until now, can a woman be entitled to exercise any public function." In *R.* v. *Harrald*, L.R. 7 Q.B. 361, a municipal election was invalidated because two married women had voted. The presiding judge, Chief Justice Cockburn, stated, "It is quite certain that, by the common law, a married woman's status, was so entirely merged in that of her husband that she was incapable of exercising almost all public functions."

Such reasoning, and indeed the exclusion of women from public office, was reconsidered in the famous "Person's Case," *Edwards* v. *Attorney General for Canada*, [1930] A.C. 124. To Lord Sankey L.C., it was "a relic of times more barbarous than ours." Lord

Sankey's refusal to follow the general (and economically attractive) opinion was not, however, unique. In 1917, the Appellate Division of the Alberta Supreme Court in *R.* v. *Cyr* (1917), 3 W.W.R. 849, had also discarded the accepted wisdom. At issue was whether a woman had the legal capacity to act as a police magistrate. Alice Jamieson, a police magistrate in Calgary, had convicted Cyr of vagrancy and a ground of appeal taken by her lawyer was that women were under a common law disability from exercising public office and, hence, Jamieson's appointment and actions as police magistrate were of no legal effect. While they considered earlier decisions and the reasoning and precedents upon which they were based, the judges in *Cyr* made a fundamentally different choice about their scope and interpretation, holding rather:

[I]n my opinion...it can be said with absolute truth that there is no actual decision to be found later than *R.* v. *Stubbs*, [1788] 2 T.R. 395 — which held that a woman could hold the public office of overseer of the poor — upon the general question of the common-law capacity of women to hold public office. There is no decision at any time declaring their incapacity. Even the dicta so declaring are by courts whose decisions are not binding upon us. These dicta, which undoubtedly rest upon practice and usage, were merely made possible by the omission of the Crown through a number of centuries to appoint women to public office, no doubt because advisers to the Crown thought them unsuitable. This is very far from establishing a legal incapacity if the advisers of the Crown here and now happen to entertain a different view as to their suitability....

I therefore think that applying the general principle upon which the common law rests, namely of reason and good sense as applied to new conditions, this Court ought to declare that in this province, and at this time in our presently existing conditions there is at common law no legal disqualification for holding public office in the government of the country arising from any distinction of sex. And in doing this, I am strongly of the opinion that we are returning to the more liberal and enlightened view of the middle ages in England and passing over the narrower and more hardened view, which possibly by the middle of the nineteenth century, had gained the

---

[16] *In Re Mabel French* (1905), 37 N.B.R. 359 at 361.

ascendancy in England. (per Stuart J. speaking for the Court, at 855–56; 858–59.)

Both the conviction and Jamieson's appointment as police magistrate were upheld. However, the *Cyr* decision is more notable for its departure from the judicial tide than as a sign of change. The Supreme Court of Canada had "reverted" to the alternate reading of the common law in 1928 when it held women ineligible to be called as senators: *Re Section 24 of the British North America Act, 1867*, [1928] S.C.R. 276. It was this decision that was appealed to the Privy Council in *Edwards* where the matter was resolved in favour of women's personhood and legal status.

ILLOGICAL BUT LAW

The mix of romanticism, maternity, ornamental wives and womanly functions also found its way into legal pronouncements on women's paid work. *Muller* v. *Oregon* 208 U.S. 412 (1908) involved a challenge made by an employer to legislation limiting the maximum hours for women employees in "any mechanical establishment, or factory, or laundry" to ten hours a day. The employer argued that this interfered with the freedom of the contract of employment. In rejecting the challenge to the legislation, Justice Brewer in the U.S. Supreme Court commented:

> that women's physical structure and the performance of maternal functions place her at a disadvantage in the struggle for subsistence is obvious. This is especially true when the burdens of motherhood are upon her. Even when they are not, by abundant testimony of the medical fraternity [sic], continuance for a long time on her feet at work, repeating this from day to day, tends to injurious effects upon the body, and as healthy mothers are essential to vigorous offspring, the physical well-being of women becomes an object of public interest, and care in order to preserve the strength and vigour of the race. Still again, history discloses that woman has always been dependent upon man. There is that in her disposition and habits of life which will operate against a full assertion (of her rights to be educated or to earn a living).... Her physical structure and a proper discharge of her maternal functions...justify legislation to protect her from the greed as well as the passion of man...the reason...rests in the inherent difference in the sexes and in

the different functions in life which they perform. (at 422–423)

These ideas of "inherent difference" or of "respect and decorum" and the "civilized order," directing a special "privilege" of exclusion (or less favourable treatment) from the public sphere will be encountered again. But, it should be noted that they are not just a legacy of the late nineteenth or early twentieth century. It is possible to find similar reasoning in the 1968 case of *Beckett* v. *City of Sault Ste. Marie Police Commissioners* 67 D.L.R. (2d) 286. In this case, a woman police officer objected to being paid less than male police officers with identical duties. The judge, Ferguson J. rejected her complaint as ill-founded. After noting that she "was single and had no family obligations whatever," he added that being a policewoman constable did not of itself entitle her to the same pay as the male constables. "She is not being discriminated against by the fact that she receives a different wage, for the fact of the difference is in accord with every rule of economics, civilization, family life and common sense." (at 294) On appeal, the parties agreed to arbitration. It should be noted, however, that Scroeder J.A. commented in the appeal decision that Ferguson J.'s comments were a "sweeping generalization" to which he did not assent.[17]

In 1973, the U.S. Supreme Court considered these sex classifications in a case involving dependent's benefits for servicemen and women. In *Frontiero* v. *Richardson* 411 U.S. 677 (1973) at 682, Justice Brennan stated: "there can be no doubt that our nation has a long and unfortunate history of sex discrimination. Traditionally, such discrimination was rationalized by an attitude of 'romantic paternalism' which, in practical effect, put women, not on a pedestal, but in a cage."

Other examples of judicial constructions of women, women's roles and their interaction with law are distributed through case reports. One notorious example is the 1978 decision of the Supreme Court of Canada on the interpretation and scope of section 1 of the Bill of Rights. In the case of *Bliss* v. *Attorney General for Canada*, [1979] 1 S.C.R. 183; 92 D.L.R. (3d) 417, the issue was whether the *Unemployment Insurance Act* which restricted the eligibility of pregnant women to UIC benefits constituted sex discrimination. Mr. Justice Ritchie rejected Stella Bliss's argument that this was sex discrimination. He acknowledged that the Act imposed conditions on women which did not apply to men but, he explained, "any inequality between the sexes in this area is not created by legislation but by nature." This improbable logic also persuaded him that

---

[17] Beckett v. City of Sault Ste Marie Police Commissioners, [1968] 2 O.R. 653, 654. (Ontario Court of Appeal).

if legislation "treated unemployed pregnant women differently from other unemployed persons, be they male or female, it is...because they are pregnant and not because they are women." (at 422)

THE CROWNING GLORY

Two sexual discrimination cases decided by the English Court of Appeal contain some particularly colourful language in relation to gender. In *Peake* v. *Automotive Products Ltd.*, [1978] 1 All E.R. 106 and in *Jeremiah* v. *Ministry of Defence*, [1979] 1 All E.R. 833, the U.K. *Sex Discrimination Act 1975* was under consideration. In *Peake*, a male employee complained that a work practice of permitting women to leave the factory five minutes earlier than the men "in the interests of safety," amounted to sex discrimination against him. Lord Denning M.R., then senior judge of the English Court of Appeal, rejected his complaint and in doing so, commented:

> Although the 1975 Act applies equally to men as to women, I must say that it would be very wrong to my mind if this Act were thought to obliterate the differences between men and women or to do away with the chivalry and courtesy which we expect mankind to give to womankind. The natural differences between the sexes must be regarded even in the interpretation of an Act of Parliament. Applied to this case, it seems to me that, when a working rule is made differentiating between men and women in the interests of safety, there is no discrimination contrary to (the Act). Instances were put before us in the course of argument, such as a cruise liner which employs both men and women. Would it be wrong to have a regulation: "Women and children first"? Or in the case of a factory in case of fire? As soon as instances are considered, the answer is clear. It is not discrimination for mankind to treat womankind with the courtesy and chivalry which we have been taught to believe is right conduct in our society.... If this be wrong...I would say that the discrimination is perfectly harmless. (at 108, 110)

Lord Denning's views were also evident in *Jeremiah*. In this case, a man alleged that he was being discriminated against on the basis of sex at his place of work. It was a practice in the ordnance factory in question that women who volunteered to do overtime were not required to work in the colour-bursting shops because of the dirty conditions and lack of protective clothing and showers for women. This, he argued, was a detriment to him to which women were not

subjected. At the initial hearing before a tribunal, the practice was declared to be unlawful and this declaration was upheld by the Court of Appeal. In commencing his judgement, Lord Denning MR said: "A woman's hair is her crowning glory, so it is said. She does not like to have it disturbed, especially when she has just had a 'hair-do'. The women at an ordnance factory in Wales are no exception. They do not want to work in a part of the factory, called a 'shop' which ruins their 'hair-do'." (at 835) He continued, "[n]ow, Mr. Jeremiah, has little regard for chivalry or for the women's hair-dos. He is a modern man. He says that there should be equality between the sexes...." Nevertheless, he appeared to retreat from *Peake* commenting that "on reconsideration, the only sound ground (in *Peake*) was that the discrimination was *de minimus*. ...the other ground (about chivalry an administrative practice) should no longer be relied upon." (at 835, 836–7)

Lord Brightman supported Lord Denning's preference that the work should be voluntary for either sex and began his decision with the following words:

> It is obviously reasonable that women, who are more concerned with, and devote more time and attention to, their personal appearance than men, should not be required by their employer to work in the atmosphere of the place so graphically described as the colour-bursting shop; and should not have to scrub themselves down under a shower and reset their hair before leaving the factory premises at the end of the day's work. The evidence suggests that women might not volunteer for overtime at all if this would necessitate their doing a compulsory stint in the colour-bursting shop.
>
> Whether a woman would be allowed to work in the colour-bursting shop if she so wished and would then be given the necessary cleaning facilities, is not clear on the evidence. The point has not yet arisen, and the answer is irrelevant to the decision in this case. (at 840)

A MACHISMO PRINCIPLE IN LAW, OR WHAT'S A REAL MAN SUPPOSED TO DO?

These attitudes find their way into judicial pronouncements and, indeed, into legal rules, although they are not unchallenged. In part this is what is meant when references are made to law being "gendered." The quotations which follow, are from recent Canadian judgements. They combine judicial views of women, with (perhaps unintended) insights into how these views can be translated into, or reflected by, legal rules and standards.

In 1977, a 21-year-old man was convicted of a charge of unlawfully confining an eighteen-year-old woman. The accused allegedly went to a house with a knife in his hand, broke down a door, ripped the telephone off the wall, and forcibly seized the woman. He was on probation for similar offences at the time of these events. He was sentenced to six months in prison. The trial judge, Judge Bewley, made the following comments about the young woman and her friends, during the trial:

There is a girl here, or a couple of girls, young nubile females, who've been around a bit, eh? They've travelled from Ontario to here, they're a free floating type of female, young for their age, very nubile, very attractive, surely, but, I suppose, basically I have to look at it this way, still impressionable, still stupid...you know women don't get much brains before they're thirty anyway...but at the age of eighteen or so, they make some stupid mistakes, mostly because we males who know better, lead them into it.

...I found him technically guilty of unlawful confinement, you know, but I'm not too sympathetic towards these stupid girls. There's no big deal, right? It isn't as if he held up a __ as in the other case, where he may have held up an innocent driver, getting away from something or threatened a policeman with a knife or something. He's demonstrating his manhood to a little girl eighteen years of age, who's probably half inclined to think he's a man by showing a knife, so big deal, eh?

So, I could give him five years, but I don't think under the circumstances of this case, I'd be entitled to give him five years, because as we clearly have said before, he got mixed up with a silly, little bunch of girls who mean well, they got scared because he was proving himself a macho man, was going to haul one of them out and talk to her even if she got scared and ran into the bedroom, so we've got a bunch of clucking females running around, and they are all so scared that they have to call the Police.[18]

A question on the constitutionality of restrictions regarding the admission of evidence of prior sexual conduct with persons other than the accused in a sexual assault trial, gave rise to the following reflec-

tions on the rules of evidence by Mr. Justice Marshall in *R. v. Oquataq*:

Although relating chastity to likelihood of consent is unfair, it has comprised part of the carefully balanced evidentiary process.... The question of the proper evaluation of such evidence is a difficult one. It is a question of logic — what is legally relevant, what is logically probative of the issues with which we are dealing.... Now then, in logic, is willingness to consent to have intercourse outside of marriage or established relationships...is [such] sexual indulgence logically probative of consent on a particular occasion? ...Does it mean, the girl [sic] was more likely to have consented? It is logically probative. The problem with this assumption is that it denies both autonomy and dignity to women...[but] our test for judicial truth is based on probabilities...it may show rank prejudice; but we use it.[19]

Rank prejudice need not be limited to the rules themselves as illustrated by comments made by Judge Denys Dionne, during an assault and weapons trial in the Montreal suburb of Longueuil. The remark was made on January 27, 1989, but only came to light early in 1990. *The [Toronto] Globe and Mail* reported on February 13, 1990, that "Judge Dionne interjected in an argument over a point of law and said: 'Rules are like women, they are made to be violated.'" A lawyer involved in the case responded: "Exactly." An official complaint against the judge was made by the Quebec Ministry of Justice to the Quebec Judicial Council, pending which the judge was suspended. At the hearing into his conduct in April,

the judge told the five-member panel of the Quebec Judicial Council that the remark was made sarcastically to dismiss an argument advanced by a defence lawyer. An audio recording of the remark played in the courtroom revealed that a lawyer was stressing how "all good principles of law have their exceptions" when Dionne interjected with the comment. "It was to make him (the defence lawyer) understand through an absurdity the irrational nature of his argument."

Suzanne Boivin, a lawyer for two women's groups represented at the hearing, asked Dionne about a 1988 incident in which he made a similar remark while presiding over a

---

[18] *R. v. Tourangeau* (25 August 1977) (Prov. Ct. B.C.). See further, Elizabeth Atcheson, Mary Eberts and Elizabeth Symes, *Women and Legal Action* (Ottawa: CACSW, 1984) at 40–42.
[19] Marshall J. in *R. v. Oquataq* (1985), 18 C.C.C. (3d) 440 at 450 (N.W.T.).

trial in Sherbrooke, Quebec. Dionne said he didn't recall the incident. Handed a transcript of the trial, he said he had sought to qualify the comment by prefacing it with the words: "As you know there are many who say things like." Similarly, the 1989 comment which led to the inquiry was preceded by the words: "As they say..." Dionne said the attempt to qualify the statement showed that the comments did not represent his personal point of view. Dionne testified to the panel which oversees the conduct of judges in the province that he first heard the controversial remark about 30 years ago from a respected Quebec jurist. Since then, he said, he has heard the comment only two or three times. Boivin also quoted from a divorce hearing Dionne presided over in Sherbrooke in 1989 where the judge made comments extolling the virtues of the traditional family.

Dionne — a former deputy minister in the provincial justice department — apologized to those who may have felt offended or hurt by his remark. But Dianne Lemieux, spokesman for the two women's groups, rejected Dionne's apology, saying the comment was unacceptable regardless of the context. In earlier testimony, Crown prosecutor Michel Breton, who was in court when Dionne uttered the 1989 comment, said he considered the remark a "farce" or a "quip" made in impatience to the defence lawyer. "It was something I've heard before," testified Breton. "I was not surprised and I didn't notice any surprise in the courtroom."[20]

On June 29, 1990, the report of the disciplinary committee was made public. It ruled that the comment was "sexist, in extremely bad taste and unacceptable coming from a judge. It also said that the comments tarnished the image of justice and could lead people to believe that some judges are prejudiced and incapable of rendering impartial decisions." The secretary of the Quebec Judicial Council, indicated that Dionne would be severely reprimanded but not removed from the bench. He also said that the goal of the reprimand would be to make sure that the judge realized such statements were wrong and would not be tolerated. On July 3, 1990, the Canadian Press Newswire reported that Dionne "got a stern dressing-down in private from Chief Judge Albert Gobeil, as ordered by the Quebec Judicial Council after a disciplinary hearing. He can now return to the bench after a four-month suspension."

Such incidents should not be regarded as isolated or aberrant. In December 1989, Judge Bourassa, a territorial court judge in the Northwest Territories, was quoted by the *Edmonton Journal* as saying, "The majority of rapes in the Northwest Territories occur when the woman is drunk and passed out. A man comes along and sees a pair of hips and helps himself. That contrasts sharply to the cases I dealt with before (as a judge in southern Canada) of the dainty co-ed who gets jumped from behind."[21]

The judge later said that he regretted his remarks. Pending the conclusion of a public inquiry called by the Territorial Judicial Council in February 1990 to investigate his conduct, Judge Bourassa was assigned to administrative duties. At the end of September 1990, Madame Justice Conrad, who conducted the public inquiry, recommended that no disciplinary action be taken against Bourassa. In 1984, Judge Bourassa was also the focus of a storm of controversy over his sentencing of three Inuit men who pleaded guilty to a charge of sexually assaulting a 13-year-old mentally impaired girl. He gave the men one-week jail terms "because the Inuit of the Eastern Arctic do not recognize an age of consent," and because the accused men were "upstanding community members." His decision was appealed, with a four-month term being substituted by the Court of Appeal.[22] This lenient sentencing appears to be part of a pattern in the Northwest Territories. It is in stark contrast both to the applicable minimum sentencing guideline of three years' imprisonment for major sexual assault,[23] and to sentences of 8–10 years' imprisonment which have been given where an accused is aboriginal and the victim is non-aboriginal.[24]

Judge Mark De Weerdt of the Northwest Territories Supreme Court ruled that "a man who beat his wife deserved a lighter sentence because she provoked him by wearing a lewd T-shirt. The shirt, showing cartoon polar bears engaged in sex-acts, could be seen as "implying the possibility, if not the actual

---

[20] Eric Siblin, 11 April 1990, *Canadian Press Newswire*.

[21] Edmonton Journal, (20 December 1989).

[22] *R. v. Curley, Naqmalik and Issigaitok*, [1984] N.W.T.R. 281 (C.A.), rev'g [1984] N.W.T.R. 263 (T.C.).

[23] *R. v. Sandercock* (1985), 22 C.C.C. (3d) 84.

[24] Eg. *R. v. Amyot*, [1987] N.W.T.R. 337; *R. v. Beaulieu* (1986) N.W.T.J. no. 113 (Q.L.). See generally Teressa Ann Nahanee, "Criminal Law: The Impact of Race, Judicial Discretion and Disparity on Sentencing in Major Sexual Assault Cases: Do Lenient Sentences Deny Inuit Females Their Section 7 and Section 15 Constitutional Rights to Personal Security and Equal Treatment Under Law" (Prepared for Pauktuutit — Inuit Women's Association, Ottawa 1990).

promise of sexual perversity and promiscuity".... In his ruling, De Weerdt said the T-shirt's implication "could be understood by the other spouse as an imminent threat that she might commit adultery." Such a threat would be "calculated to arouse alarm, fear, and anger in that other spouse, with clearly foreseeable consequences," he said.[25] Instead of a prison sentence, the judge imposed a fine of $1,000. His decision has also been appealed.

In other examples of concern to women, it is possible to note a shift from what we might now view as blatant, explicit bias to a more subtle form of bias. Judges may use existing definitions or follow the logic of existing reasoning to reach a result — but the reasoning on which it is based excludes the experiences or understandings of women. Four examples of this can be given. The Manitoba Court of Appeal held that to consider sexual harassment to be sex discrimination was "amazing." Rather, the judges opined, if not all women in a workplace were harassed, the attention given to some women must be because they are attractive, not because they are women.[26] The same court rejected a defence of self-defence raised to a homicide charge by a battered woman, referring to it as "fanciful."[27] The New Brunswick Court of Appeal held that touching a woman's breast should not be considered a sexual assault. The judges reasoned that breasts are secondary sexual characteristics, just as a man's beard is a secondary sexual characteristic. Thus, they reasoned, only the touching of genitalia should be considered "sexual assault" to avoid "absurdity." The judges also wished to preserve the ability of men to "steal a goodnight kiss" without being vulnerable to a sexual assault charge.[28] Finally, a trial court judge acquitted a man charged with threatening serious bodily harm. The accused had written explicit letters to cheerleaders of a football team, in which he had made it clear that he knew where they lived and that he would have sexual intercourse with them, even if he had to rape them. The trial judge held that this was not a threat to cause serious bodily harm.[29] (It should also be noted that these particular decisions were reversed on appeal.)

AN UPDATE: RECENT EXAMPLES

Concerns about comments (and conduct) by Canadian judges continue to be raised. Some instances which have attracted media attention include:

- October 1992: During a discussion in his office, Leonard Blackburn, a Justice of the Peace, told a teenager that she had "a great body"; on another occasion, a private investigator who was attending court to lay two charges of theft, complained that Blackburn had made speculative comments about her pubic hair and rubbed her hand when she put it on a Bible to swear an oath. An inquiry, undertaken in December 1992 by Provincial Court Judge Mary Hogan and tabled in the legislature in February 1993, recommended that he no longer continue to work as a JP.

- September 1993: Judge Frank Allen, a Manitoba provincial court judge, received a reprimand from the Manitoba Judicial Council in relation to a range of remarks dating back to 1985 when he had commented, while sentencing a man who had threatened to kill his former girlfriend and himself, "I can tell you from 60-odd years of experience that there isn't any woman worth the trouble you got yourself into." In 1989, Judge Allen reprimanded a female lawyer who was seeking an adjournment because her nursing infant was running an extremely high fever and throwing up antibiotics. The lawyer was herself unwell. The judge suggested that she find a replacement "who is not trying to be a mother and a lawyer at the same time". The Council concluded that judges don't have the right to make sexist comments, but that Judge Allen's remarks did not prove that he was incompetent.

- November 1993: Judge Rene Crochetiere ruled that there was insufficient evidence to order a trial for a man accused of threatening to kill his common-law wife. The woman commented to the judge that if she were to be killed "it will be your fault." The judge replied, "I would like to tell everyone here that if ever this man kills this woman, it won't stop me from sleeping and I won't die — don't worry, I won't get depressed either. It wasn't my responsibility." Following a complaint to the Quebec Judicial Council, Judge Crocheterie was severely reprimanded for his remarks.

- Fall 1993: Judge Walter Hryciuk, a provincial court judge was ordered removed from the bench for sexual misconduct following an inquiry into allegations by two female Crown attorneys that he had sexually harassed and touched them. The

---

[25] *The [Toronto] Saturday Star*, (15 July, 1990) A1.
[26] *Janzen v. Platy Enterprises* (1986), 43 Man. R. (2d) 293.
[27] *R. v. Lavellee* (1988), 52 Man. R. (2d) 274.
[28] *R. v. Chase* (1984), 40 C.R. (3d) 282.
[29] *R. v. McGraw* (November 8, 1988) (Dist. Ct. Ont., Flanagan, D.C.J.) Also reproduced in (1989) 21 Ottawa L.Rev. 201.

allegations included that the judge had made lewd remarks, and had forced his tongue into one of the women's mouths during an unwanted kiss. (See *Ontario Commission of Inquiry into the Conduct of His Honour Judge W.P. Hryciuk*, Released November 24, 1993.) In May 1994, the Ontario Divisional Court rejected an appeal by the judge, related to the process of the Inquiry ([1994] 18 O.R. (3d) 695).

- December 1993: Manitoba Circuit Court Judge Bruce MacDonald resigned prior to the commencement of an inquiry by the Manitoba Judicial Council into his conduct over a 20-year period. The inquiry was discontinued. However, media reports suggest that MacDonald had made the following comments during his work as a judge: In 1969, he stated, "it would be a joyful result" if residents of an Indian reserve "killed each other off." No action was taken. In 1987, he remarked to a man convicted of sexually abusing his daughter that he should have hired a prostitute instead. Complaints arising from this remark led to a private reprimand. In 1993, the judge gave a suspended sentence to a man convicted of sexually assaulting four female relatives. He commented that the man was "just curious" when he committed the offences. It was after this remark that a judicial inquiry was ordered. Following the judge's resignation and the cancellation of the inquiry, questions were raised as to why the numerous concerns about MacDonald over the years had not led to effective action or intervention.

- May 1994: The Supreme Court of Canada reversed a Nova Scotia Court of Appeal decision which had ruled that if a woman does not resist a sexual assault, she is consenting to it (*R.* v. *M.L.M.*, [1994] 2 S.C.R. 3).

- June 1994: The Quebec Judicial Council dismissed as unfounded the complaints against Judge Raymonde Verrault. In the course of sentencing a stepfather for sodomising his infant stepdaughter, Judge Verrault had remarked that it was a mitigating factor that the father had preserved his daughter's virginity, which is important in Muslim culture.

Against the backdrop of these individual examples are various institutional responses. In addition to provincial judicial councils which investigate complaints against provincially appointed judges, the Canadian Judicial Council investigates complaints against federally appointed judges. In 1991–92, the Council received 115 complaints. It made no recommendations for removal of judges. It publicly disapproved of two judges' actions and two judges resigned because complaints were heard.

In 1992, the Canadian Bar Association (CBA) initiated a Task Force to inquire into gender bias in the legal profession. This task force was chaired by the retired Supreme Court Justice, Hon. Bertha Wilson. In its fair-ranging report, the task force recommended, *inter alia*, parental leave policies for female and male lawyers, flexible work arrangements, workplace equity, sexual harassment policies, commissions to investigate gender-based complaints against judges and mandatory courses on gender and racial bias for all newly appointed and sitting judges. Following the submission of the Task Force Report, the CBA passed a resolution at its meetings of February 1994 recognizing inequalities in the legal profession and initiated a process directed toward establishing a similar inquiry into racism in the legal profession.

In February 1994, the Center for Research Action on Race Relations, a Montreal-based group, established a courtwatch in response to criticism that Quebec's judges are insensitive to the many cultures which come before them in courtrooms. All the 480 Quebec judges are white, except for one judge who is aboriginal. About 13 per cent of them are women.

In 1988, Ontario established a Judicial Appointments Committee which solicits applications from under-represented groups whenever there is a vacancy on the provincial court bench. The Committee is made up of five lawyers and four laypeople. Between 1988 and 1994, the Committee has appointed 90 people — 39 of whom are women; 12, people of colour; and 6, francophone. Ontario has 260 provincial court judges. The committee was permanently established via a statute in June 1994. There are approximately 276 federally appointed judges in Ontario, 32 of whom are women.

REFLECTIONS

Certain themes echo throughout the material woven together in this section. It seems many judges and others have had (surprising) difficulty with women as women, in relation to sexuality, reproduction, social roles, etc. Indeed, efforts have been made to "construct" or create a formal or official view of women. While recalling that law is not monolithic and contradictions within it are apparent, comments by Carol Smart, a feminist sociologist of law are thought-provoking. She has suggested that

> where chaotic female bodies enter, it is presumed that meaningful, rationale behaviour stops...it is assumed that where bodies are, minds are not.... Law has been part of a process of providing quite specific cultural

meanings to women's bodies...moreover, law has sexualized women's bodies and rendered them unreliable and too prone to nature.[30]

Luce Irigary and Zillah Eisenstein have further suggested that

the presence of women seems impossible to imagine within law as it is presently formed. "That would not fail to challenge the discourse that lays down the law today, that legislates on everything, including sexual difference, to such an extent that the existence of another sex, of another, that would be woman, still seems, in its terms, unimaginable.".... [T]he only way to create space for women is to develop a new language, one which no longer assumes that men are "everything" — "that [the masculine] could no longer, all by itself, define, circumvent, circumscribe, the properties of any thing and everything."[31]

Another (startling) point is that some judges and commenters, continue to speak in a vein similar to their forerunners. The "comfort zone" of thinking of such outbursts as the product of another century, "but things are different now and women are equal," seems to be misleading. What has changed is that accountability for such statements has increased and judicial education programs have been established to address the problem and enable judges to perform their duties in a way that is more impartial and just.

Several questions are posed by the material in this section. It is instructive to note how abstracted and formalized a view of women has, at times, been articulated by judges. Where is the experience of working class women, or aboriginal women or non-White women? How significant is their absence? To what extent is there a similar limited construction of women (and men) in legal discourse today? To what extent is there a similar resistance to changes in societal (and legal) roles for women (and men) today?

Are there internal safeguards in the judicial appeal structure to prevent or redress the effects of gender bias? Is it possible that fundamental change in the structure of legal analysis and legal rules can occur with effective advocacy? (That is, by making the right arguments in court.) Or, is a change necessary in structures, discourses and worldviews? How can arguments and worldviews be changed? What is the role of law in reflecting social changes and how effective are legal pronouncements in redressing disadvantages in women's social, economic and legal position? Indeed, how important is law as we address fundamental social problems of inequality?

---

[30] Carol Smart, *Feminism and the Power of Law* (London: Routledge, 1989) at 93, 103. Compare with Chief Justice Neaves in *Jex-Blake v. Edinburgh Medical School* (1869): "It is a belief, widely entertained that there is great difference in the mental constitution of the two sexes, just as there is in their physical conformation. The powers and susceptibilities of women are as noble as those of men; but they are thought to be different, and, in particular, it is considered that they have not the same power of intense labour as men are endowed with. If this be so, it must form serious objection to uniting them under the same course of academic study."

[31] Zillah Eisenstein, *The Female Body and the Law* (Berkeley: University of California Press, 1988) at 54; citing Luce Irigary, *This Sex Which is Not One*, Catherine Porter [trans.] with Carolyn Burke, (Ithaca, NY: Cornell University Press, 1985) at 80, 85.

2. Historical Markers: A Brief Chronology of Women and the Law

This chronology* highlights some of the significant events in the legal position and the struggles of Canadian women. Occasionally, references are made to occurrences outside of Canada which are considered to be relevant or of related interest to Canadian women.

The following sources were of particular relevance in compiling the chronology:

Altschul, S. and C. Carron, "Chronology of Some of the Legal Landmarks in the History of Canadian Women," (1975) 21 McGill L.J. 476.

Armour, Moira, *Canadian Women in History: A Chronology*. Toronto: Green Dragon, 1990.

Braithwaite, Rella, *The Black Woman in Canada*. Toronto: OISE, 1976.

Crossing the Bar: A Century of Women's Experience "Upon the Rough and Troubled Seas of Legal Practice" in Ontario, The Law Society of Upper Canada Archives, Toronto, 1993.

MacLaren, Sherill, *Invisible Power: The Women Who Run Canada*. Toronto: Seal Books, 1991.

Vickers, Jill, Pauline Rankin, and Christine Appelle, *Politics as If Women Mattered: A Political Analysis of the National Action Committee on the Status of Women*. Toronto: University of Toronto Press, 1993.

See also:

Atcheson, Elizabeth, Mary Eberts, and Elizabeth Symes, *Women and Legal Action*. Ottawa: CACSW, 1984.

Boivin, Michelle, "L'evolution des droits de la femme au Quebec: un sorvol historique" (1986) 2 Can J. of Women and the Law 53–68.

Report of the Royal Commission on the Status of Women in Canada, 1970.

Sachs, Albie and Joan Hoff-Wilson, *Sexism in Law*. London: Martin Robertson, 1978.

---

* Jennifer Quaile provided excellent research assistance in revising this section of the book, to update, adjust and expand the materials included.

1765

Blackstone, a legal commentator who attempted to systematize the body of English Common Law to enable it to be more accessible to lay people, sum- marised the legal effects of marriage at the time of his writing in the following way.

Commentaries on the Laws of England*

...Having thus shewn how marriages may be made, or dissolved, I come now, lastly, to speak of the legal conse- quences of such making, or dissolution.

By marriage, the husband and wife are one person in law: that is, the very being on legal existence of the woman is suspended during the marriage, or at least is incorporated and consolidated into that of the husband; under whose wing, protection, and *cover* she performs every thing; and is therefore called in our law — french a *feme-covert, foemina viro co-operta*; is said to be *covert-baron*, or under the protection and influence of her husband, her *baron*, or lord; and her condition during her marriage is called her *coverture*. Upon this principle, of an union of person in husband and wife, depend almost all the legal rights, duties, and disabilities, that either of them acquire by the marriage. I speak not at present of the rights of property, but of such as are merely *personal*. For this reason, a man cannot grant anything to his wife, or enter into covenant with her: for the grant would be to suppose her separate existence; and to covenant with her, would be only to covenant with himself: and therefore it is also generally true, that all compacts made between husband and wife, when single, are voided by the intermarriage. A woman indeed may be attorney for her husband; for that implies no separation from, but is rather a representation of, her lord. And a husband may also bequeath any thing to his wife by will; for that cannot take effect till the coverture is determined by his death. The husband is bound to provide his wife with necessaries by law, as much as himself; and, if she contracts debts for them, he is obliged to pay them; but for any thing besides necessaries he is not chargeable. Also if a wife elopes, and lives with another man, the husband is not chargeable even for necessaries; at least if the person who furnishes them is sufficiently apprized of her elopement. If the wife be indebted before marriage, the husband is bound afterwards to pay the debt; for he has adopted her and her circumstances together. If the wife be injured in her person or her property, she can bring no action for redress without her husband's concurrence, and in his name, as well as her own: neither can she be sued without making the husband a defendant. There is indeed one case where the wife shall sue and be sued as a feme sole, viz. where the husband has abjured the realm, or is banished, for then

he is dead in law; and, the husband being thus disabled to sue for or defend the wife, it would be most unreasonable if she had no remedy, or could make no defence at all. In criminal prosecutions, it is true, the wife may be indicted and punished separately; for the union is only a civil union. But in trials of any sort they are not allowed to be evidence for, or against, each other: partly because it is impossible their testimony should be indifferent, but principally because of the union of person; and therefore, if they were admitted to be witnesses *for* each other, they would contradict one maxim of law, "*nemo in propria causa testis esse debet*"; and if *against* each other, they would contradict another maxim, "*nemo tenetur seipsum accusare.*" But, where the offence is directly against the person of the wife, this rule has been usually dispensed with; and therefore, by statute 3 Hen. VII. c. 2, in case a woman be forcibly taken away, and married, she may be a witness against such her husband, in order to convict him of felony. For in this case she can with no propriety be reckoned his wife; because a main ingredient, her consent, was wanting to the contract: and also there is another maxim of law, that no man shall take advantage of his own wrong; which the ravisher here would do, if, by forcibly marrying a woman, he could prevent her from being a witness, who is perhaps the only witness to that very fact.

In the civil law the husband and the wife are considered as two distinct persons, and may have separate estates, contracts, debts, and injuries; and therefore in our ecclesi- astical courts, a woman may sue and be sued without her husband.

But though our law in general considers man and wife as one person, yet there are some instances in which she is separately considered; as inferior to him, and acting by his compulsion. And therefore all deeds executed, and acts done, by her, during her coverture, are void; except it be a fine, or the like matter of record, in which case she must be solely and secretly examined, to learn if her act be voluntary. She cannot by will devise lands to her husband, unless under special circumstances; for at the time of making it she is supposed to be under his coercion. And in some felonies, and other inferior crimes, committed by her, through constraint of her husband, the law excuses her: but this extends not to treason or murder.

---

* W. Blackstone, *Commentaries on the Laws of England, Book I*, Chapter 15, pp. 442–45.

The husband also, by the old law, might give his wife moderate correction. For, as he is to answer for her misbehaviour, the law thought it reasonable to intrust him with this power of restraining her, by domestic chastisement, in the same moderation that a man is allowed to correct his apprentices or children; for whom the master or parent is also liable in some cases to answer. But this power of correction was confined within reasonable bounds, and the husband was prohibited from using any violence to his wife, *aliter quam ad virum, ex causa regiminis et castigationis uxoris suoe, licite et rationabiliter pertinet.* The civil law gave the husband the same, or a larger, authority over his wife: allowing him, for some misdemeanors, *flagellis et fustibus acriter verberare uxorem*; for others, only *modicam castigationem adhibere.* But with us, in the politer reign of Charles the second, this power of correction began to be doubted; and a wife may now have a security of the peace against her husband; or, in return, a husband against his wife. Yet the lower rank of people, who were always fond of the old common law, still claim and exert their ancient privilege: and the courts of law will still permit a husband to restrain a wife of her liberty, in case of any gross misbehaviour.

These are the chief legal effects of marriage during the coverture; upon which we may observe, that even the disabilities which the wife lies under are for the most part intended for her protection and benefit: so great a favourite is the female sex of the laws of England.

[Blackstone's views were not universally shared, however, as the following extract expressing resistance makes clear:]

Protest*

While we acknowledge our mutual affection by publicly assuming the relationship of husband and wife, yet in justice to ourselves and a great principle, we deem it a duty to declare that this act on our part implies no sanction of, nor promise of voluntary obedience to such of the present laws of marriage as refuse to recognize the wife as an independent, rational being, while they confer upon the husband an injurious and unnatural superiority, investing him with legal powers which no honorable man would exercise and which no man should possess. We protest especially against the laws which give the husband:

1. The custody of the wife's person.
2. The exclusive control and guardianship of their children.
3. The sole ownership of her personal and use of her real estate, unless previously settled upon her, or placed in the hands of trustees, as in the case of minors, lunatics and idiots.
4. The absolute right to the product of her industry.
5. Also against laws which give to the widower so much larger and more permanent an interest in the property of his deceased wife than they give to the widow in that of the deceased husband.
6. Finally, against the whole system by which "the legal existence of the wife is suspended during marriage"

so that, in most States, she neither has a legal part in the choice of her residence, nor can she make a will, nor sue or be sued in her own name, nor inherit property.

We believe that personal independence and equal human rights can never be forfeited except for crime; that marriage should be an equal and permanent partnership, and so recognized by law; that until it is so recognized, married partners should provide against the radical injustice of present laws, by every means in their power.

We believe that where domestic difficulties arise, no appeal should be made to legal tribunals under existing laws but that all difficulties should be submitted to the equitable adjustment of arbitrators mutually chosen.

Thus reverencing law, we enter our protest against rules and customs which are unworthy of the name, since they violate justice, the essence of law.

Worcester Spy, 1855   (Signed) Henry B. Blackwell
Lucy Stone

[Note: Lucy Stone kept her birth last name after her marriage. Reaction to this then controversial choice led to the coining of the phrase "a Stoner," to refer to women who kept their last names upon marriage.]

---

* "Marriage of Lucy Stone Under Protest" (1855) in *History of Woman Suffrage, Vol. I*, (Rochester, N.Y., 1881) [as read and signed at the wedding].

1831

Legislation was passed in Lower Canada to provide that land must be disposed according to the law in England, which at this time did not recognize the right of a married woman to hold property. Since the right to vote in a legislative assembly was contingent on certain property requirements, this Act severely restricted the right of women to vote in such an election. (*An Act for rendering valid Conveyances of Lands and Other immoveable property held in Free or Common Socage within the Province of Lower Canada, and for other purposes therein mentioned*, 9 Geo. IV, c. 77.)

1837

Samuel Mosely, a fugitive slave who had escaped from Kentucky by stealing a horse, was arrested and placed in Niagara's jail after a request for his extradition to the United States was made. Several hundred black men and women living in the area encircled the building to prevent Mosely's transfer. Women were particularly involved in this action. When a deputy sheriff led Mosely out shackled to a wagon, a riot ensued in which the protestors, including the women, used their bodies to prevent the departure of Mosely and his police escort. In the disorder, Mosely escaped, and was later allowed to return to Niagara.

In 1844, it was estimated that there were about 44,000 Black fugitive slaves in Ontario. Slavery had been declared illegal in the British Empire, including Canada, in 1834.

[See: Janet Carnochan, "A Slave Rescue in Niagara, Sixty Years Ago," Niagara Historical Society, Paper No. 2 (1897) at 8–18; Robin Winks, *The Blacks in Canada* (Montreal: McGill-Queen's University Press, 1971) at 169–70.]

1839

In the United Kingdom, *An Act to Amend the Custody of Infants*, 2 & 3 Vict. (1839) c. 54, was passed and was the first legislation to permit married women to have some right to custody of their children after a marriage breakdown.

An Act to Amend the Custody of Infants*

The legislation granted mothers the right to appeal to a court for custody of very young children. Judges in equity were given the discretionary authority to issue an order awarding mothers access to their infant children. If the child was under seven years of age, the judge was also given the discretion to award custody to the mother. Adulterous mothers were not entitled to the benefit of the act. [This Act] became the foundation of all English and Canadian legislation on custody...counterpart legislation was enacted in Ontario in 1855.... The years 1886 and 1887 marked the legislative high-water mark for custody issues in both England and Canada. The English *Act to Amend the Law Relating to the Guardianship and Custody of Infants, 1886,* 49 & 50 Vict., c. 27 (UK), expanded the right of the mother to be appointed guardian upon her husband's death and to appoint others as guardian. The most important provision, however, related to disputes concerning custody and access between living parents...the legislation provided that the "Court could make such orders as it may think fit regarding the custody of such infant and the right of access thereto to either parent, having regard to the welfare of the infant, and to the conduct of the parents, and to the wishes as well of the mother as of the father." The Ontario legislature soon followed this lead and in 1887 enacted *An Act respecting the Guardianship of Minors*, S.O. 50 Vict., c. 21...in terms almost identical to the English statute.

---

* Constance Backhouse, "Shifting Patterns in Nineteenth-Century Custody Law" in David Flaherty, ed., *Essays in the History of Canadian Law*, vol. 1 (Toronto, ON: The Osgoode Society, 1981) at 217, 232–33. Reprinted by permission of author and publisher.

1848

In this year, the *Seneca Falls Declaration* was prepared. This Declaration is regarded as the "single most important document of the nineteenth-century [U.S.] women's movement. It was adopted at a meeting called to consider the 'social, civil, and religious condition and rights of women,' which assembled at the Wesleyan Chapel at Seneca Falls, New York, on July 19, 1848."

Seneca Falls Declaration*

We hold these truths to be self-evident: that all men and women are created equal; that they are endowed by their Creator with certain inalienable rights; that among these are life, liberty, and the pursuit of happiness; that to secure these rights governments are instituted, deriving their just powers from the consent of the governed. Whenever any form of government becomes destructive of these ends, it is the right of those who suffer from it to refuse allegiance to it, and to insist upon the institution of a new government, laying its foundation on such principles, and organizing its powers in such form, as to them shall seem likely to effect their safety and happiness. Prudence, indeed, will dictate that governments long established should not be changed for light and transient causes; and accordingly all experience hath shown that mankind are more disposed to suffer, while evils are sufferable, than to right themselves by abolishing the forms to which they were accustomed. But when a long train of abuses and usurpations, pursuing invariably the same object evinces a design to reduce them under absolute despotism, it is their duty to throw off such government, and to provide new guards for their future security. Such has been the patient sufferance of the women under this government, and such is now the necessity which constrains them to demand the equal station to which they are entitled.

The history of mankind is a history of repeated injuries and usurpations on the part of man toward woman, having in direct object the establishment of an absolute tyranny over her. To prove this, let facts be submitted to a candid world.

He has never permitted her to exercise her inalienable right to the elective franchise.

He has compelled her to submit to laws, in the formation of which she had no voice.

He has withheld from her rights which are given to the most ignorant and degraded men — both natives and foreigners.

Having deprived her of this first right of a citizen, the elective franchise, thereby leaving her without representation in the halls of legislation, he has oppressed her on all sides.

He has made her, if married, in the eye of the law, civilly dead.

He has taken from her all right in property, even to the wages she earns.

He has made her, morally, an irresponsible being, as she can commit many crimes with impunity, provided they be done in the presence of her husband. In the covenant of marriage, she is compelled to promise obedience to her husband, he becoming, to all intents and purposes, her master — the law giving him power to deprive her of her liberty, and to administer chastisement.

He has so framed the laws of divorce, as to what shall be the proper causes, and in case of separation, to whom the guardianship of the children shall be given, as to be wholly regardless of the happiness of women — the law, in all cases, going upon a false supposition of the supremacy of man, and giving all power into his hands.

After depriving her of all rights as a married woman, if single, and the owner of property, he has taxed her to support a government which recognizes her only when her property can be made profitable to it.

He has monopolized nearly all the profitable employments, and from those she is permitted to follow, she receives but a scanty remuneration. He closes against her all the avenues to wealth and distinction which he considers most honorable to himself. As a teacher of theology, medicine, or law, she is not known.

He has denied her the facilities for obtaining a thorough education, all colleges being closed against her.

He allows her in Church, as well as State, but a subordinate position, claiming Apostolic authority for her exclusion from the ministry, and, with some exceptions, from any public participation in the affairs of the Church.

He has created a false public sentiment by giving to the world a different code of morals for men and women, by which moral delinquencies which exclude women from society, are not only tolerated, but deemed of little account in man.

He has usurped the prerogative of Jehovah himself, claiming it as his right to assign for her a sphere of action, when that belongs to her conscience and to her God.

He has endeavored, in every way that he could, to destroy her confidence in her own powers, to lessen her

---

* "Declaration of Sentiments and Resolutions, Seneca Falls" in *History of Woman Suffrage, Vol. I,* (Rochester, N.Y., 1881).

self-respect, and to make her willing to lead a dependent and abject life.

Now, in view of this entire disfranchisement of one-half the people of this country, their social and religious degradation — in view of the unjust laws above mentioned, and because women do feel themselves aggrieved, oppressed, and fraudulently deprived of their most sacred rights, we insist that they have immediate admission to all the rights and privileges which belong to them as citizens of the United States.

In entering upon the great work before us, we anticipate no small amount of misconception, misrepresentation, and ridicule; but we shall use every instrumentality within our power to effect our object. We shall employ agents, circulate tracts, petition the State and National legislatures, and endeavor to enlist the pulpit and the press in our behalf. We hope this Convention will be followed by a series of Conventions embracing every part of the country.

RESOLUTIONS

Whereas, the great precept of nature is conceded to be, that "man shall pursue his own true and substantial happiness." Blackstone in his Commentaries remarks, that this law of Nature being coeval with mankind, and dictated by God himself, is of course superior in obligation to any other. It is binding over all the globe, in all countries and at all times; no human laws are of any validity if contrary to this, and such of them as are valid, derive all their force, and all their validity, and all their authority, mediately and immediately, from this original; therefore,

Resolved, That such laws as conflict, in any way, with the true and substantial happiness of woman, are contrary to the great precept of nature and of no validity, for this is "superior in obligation to any other."

Resolved, That all laws which prevent woman from occupying such a station in society as her conscience shall dictate, or which place her in a position inferior to that of man, are contrary to the great precept of nature, and therefore of no force or authority.

Resolved, That woman is man's equal — was intended to be so by the Creator, and the highest good of the race demands that she should be recognized as such.

Resolved, That the women of this country ought to be enlightened in regard to the laws under which they live, that they may no longer publish their degradation by declaring themselves satisfied with their present position, nor their ignorance, by asserting that they have all the rights they want.

Resolved, That inasmuch as man, while claiming for himself intellectual superiority, does accord to woman moral superiority, it is pre-eminently his duty to encourage her to speak and teach, as she has an opportunity, in all religious assemblies.

Resolved, That the same amount of virtue, delicacy, and refinement of behavior that is required of woman in the social state, should also be required of man, and the same transgressions should be visited with equal severity on both man and woman.

Resolved, That the objection of indelicacy and impropriety, which is so often brought against woman when she addresses a public audience, comes with a very ill-grace from those who encourage, by their attendance, her appearance on the state, in the concert, or in feats of the circus.

Resolved, That woman has too long rested satisfied in the circumscribed limits which corrupt customs and a perverted application of the Scriptures have marked out for her, and that it is time she should move in the enlarged sphere which her great Creator has assigned her.

Resolved, That it is the duty of the women of this country to secure to themselves their sacred right to the elective franchise.

Resolved, That the equality of human rights results necessarily from the fact of the identity of the race in capabilities and responsibilities.

Resolved, therefore, That, being invested by the Creator with the same capabilities, and the same consciousness of responsibility for their exercise, it is demonstrably the right and duty of woman, equally with man, to promote every righteous cause by every righteous means; and especially in regard to the great subjects of morals and religion, it is self-evidently her right to participate with her brother in teaching them, both in private and in public, by writing and by speaking, by any instrumentalities proper to be used, and in any assemblies proper to be held; and this being a self-evident truth growing out of the divinely implanted principles of human nature, any custom or authority adverse to it, whether modern or wearing the hoary sanction of antiquity, is to be regarded as a self-evident falsehood, and at war with mankind.

. . . .

Resolved, That the speedy success of our cause depends upon the zealous and untiring efforts of both men and women, for the overthrow of the monopoly of the pulpit, and for the securing to woman an equal participation with men in the various trades, professions, and commerce.

1849

An Act consolidating various legislative assembly elections Acts was passed and specifically excludes women from voting in any "County" or "Riding, City, or Town." *An Act to repeal certain Acts therein mentioned, and to amend, consolidate, and reduce into one Act, the several Statutory Provisions now in* force for the regulation of Elections of Members to Represent the People of this Province in the Legislative

Assembly thereof, 12 Vict., c. 27, s. 46 (Province of Canada).

. . . .

Harriet Tubman, a black slave in the U.S. escaped after being warned that she was about to be sold, and began her flight to freedom. She became one of the most famous "conductors" on the Underground Railroad which assisted escaped slaves travel to safety in the northern United States and into Canada. The Railroad was already established as early as 1820. Tubman made over 19 perilous trips and was proud that she had "never lost a passenger." Tubman was called the "Moses of her people" and she recalled that during her youth she was haunted a vision in which "she saw a line dividing slavery from freedom; on the

northern slope there stood people stretching their hands across the boundary to welcome her and calling her Moses." She once said: "There's two things I got a right to: and these are death and liberty. One or the other I mean to have. No one will take me back alive; I shall fight for my liberty and when the time has come for me to go, the Lord will let them kill me." She was never captured and continued to be a strong and vocal advocate for the abolition of slavery.

[See further: Charles Blockson, *The Underground Railroad* (New York: Prentice Hall, 1987) at 98–99.]

1851

The first legislation granting married women certain property rights was passed in New Brunswick, thus predating legislation in England by almost 20 years: *An Act to secure to Married Women Real and Personal Property held in their own right*. S.N.B 1851, c. 24. Other legislation followed:

- *An Act respecting certain separate rights of property of Married Women* (1859) 22 Vict., c. 73 (Ontario)

- *An Act for the Protection of Married Women in certain cases* S.N.S. 1866, c. 33
- *Married Women's Property Act*, 1870, (U.K.) 33 & 34 Vict., c. 93
- *Married Women's Property Act*, 1872, S.O. 1871–72, c. 16
- *Married Women's Property Act*, 1882, (U.K.) 45 & 46 Vict., c. 75
- *Married Women's Property Act*, 1884, S.O. 1184, c. 19

Wives and Property*

In 1869 Susannah Palmer appeared in the Recorder's Court in London, charged with stabbing her husband. After years of brutal treatment at his hands she had left him, determined to support herself and her children in a new home. But her husband had found her, and seized and sold all her possessions, which legally belonged to him. Susannah Palmer was convicted and sentenced to prison, for she was the criminal, not the adulterous husband who had beaten and robbed her. A few years after this, Millicent Garrett Fawcett had her purse snatched by a young thief in London. When she appeared in court to testify against him, she heard the youth charged with "stealing from the person of Millicent Fawcett a purse containing £1 18s. 6d., the property of Henry Fawcett." Long afterward she recalled, "I felt as if I had been charged with theft myself." Such were two women's experiences of the common law relating to married women's property. One was a poor working woman who would have

gone unnoticed in her time but for her tragic story. The other, happily married to a distinguished Cambridge professor and Liberal member of parliament, was for years one of the outstanding leaders of the women's suffrage cause in England.

The stories of women as different as these two illuminate the arguments used by Victorian feminists in their demands for reform of the married women's property law and other legal reforms as well. On the one hand, the law often inflicted grievous practical hardships upon women. On the other, the law, regarding a woman as her husband's servant, even as his chattel, destroyed her independence, her identity, and her self-respect. Reform of the common law affecting married women stands out, therefore, as a major achievement of nineteenth-century feminism.

Indeed, it can be argued that reform of the married women's property law was the most important of all the

---

* Lee Holcombe, *Wives and Property* (Toronto: University of Toronto Press, 1983) at 3–4; 50; 53–54. Reprinted by permission of University of Toronto Press.

legal reforms won by feminists in the nineteenth century. In the history of English law, property and personal status have been closely linked, and the fact that under the law married women controlled no property, their husbands exercising control instead, necessarily reduced them to a subordinate and dependent legal status, deprived of the legal rights and responsibilities of men and unmarried women. Whether spinsters or widows, unmarried women enjoyed the same rights over property as men, with the single (but major) exception that possession of property did not qualify them to vote. It was not the fact of being female but the status of wife that entailed severe legal disabilities. But the great majority of women in England did marry and lose their property, and therefore did become legally subordinate to and dependent upon their husbands. Legally deprived of property, married women were also deprived both of power and of the civil rights of other citizens.

Highly important in themselves, the legal consequences of marriage had implications for the position of women far beyond the realm of law. For example, why should women be educated and trained to work as men were? They would marry and be taken care of, along with their property, by their husbands. Why should they be encouraged to take an interest in social problems and in public affairs? As married women they would have no practical means of helping to solve the problems of their time, and would be regarded legally as merely appendages of their husbands. Why, indeed, should not society generally, women as well as men, consider women to be inferior? The law held that they were. In short, as feminists always argued, the law affecting married women was degrading to all women.

It was for these reasons that one observer of the Victorian scene declared that "the first point in the women's charter" should be reform of the married women's property law. It was not, he added caustically, "so attractive and showy a subject as are voting, and speechmaking, and public showing-off of all the usual ridiculous kind," but it had "the merit of being useful, and the still greater merit of being quite simple and practicable, although, perhaps in the eyes of the rabid women's rights fanatics, this is its least recommendation." In fact, reform of the married women's property law was "the first point in the women's charter." Feminism as an organized movement made its appearance in England in the 1850s, and the feminists of this time, dedicated to winning reform of the laws affecting women, set as their first priority reform of the laws relating to the property of married women.

. . . .

The question of why movements for social reform arise when they do and why they succeed or fail is perennially fascinating to historians. They happily construct models and write equations to subsume and give coherence to the particular historical data at their disposal, and to serve as a key to the understanding of social reform movements in general. To judge by the beginnings of feminism as an organized movement in England in the 1850s, the following seem to be necessary for the appearance and success of reform movements: economic discontent; political unrest, arising from such developments as the discrediting of the government in power or the emergence of a particular problem to be solved through the political process; the presence of leading personalities to voice economic and political discontents, to educate and to arouse the conscience of the public about the reform desired, and to present a philosophy of change; and some effective organization or machinery to push the reform through the appropriate channels. All of these parts of the model, all of these factors in the equation, were present in the England of the 1850s to account for the rise of a feminist movement which had as its first priority reform of the married women's property law.

1853

Between 1853–1857, the *Provincial Freeman* was published in Ontario, and promoted an anti-slavery campaign. The editor, and later owner of the newspaper, was Mary Ann Shadd who also helped to organize the Anti-Slavery Society of Canada. In 1853, Mary Ann Shadd became the first black woman known to have lectured in public in Canada (Armour, p. 11).

In 1855, when Lucy Stone, a well-known U.S. feminist addressed "crowded audiences on the subject of women's rights," Shadd wrote in her editorial that she was "encouraged that in Toronto, with the strong attachment to antiquated notions respecting women and her sphere, so prevalent, she was listened to patiently, applauded abundantly, and patronized extensively." (Jim Beardon and Linda Jean Butler, *Shadd: The Life and Times of Mary Shadd Cary* [Toronto: NC Press, 1977], pp. 160–161. See also Braithwaite, p. 12.)

1866

The Civil Code of Lower Canada came into being. Among its provisions were contained the following: a married woman was legally incapable of entering a contract or of appearing before the courts (art. 986); she could not engage in a calling distinct from that of her husband, nor engage in commerce without his consent (art. 181); in community of property, only the husband could administer and dispose of the joint property (art. 1292), while in separation of property, the wife could administer but not dispose of her own property (arts. 1422, 1424); mothers had a right to supervise and correct children only if the father defaulted (art. 245).

1872

Ontario enacted the *Married Women's Property Act, 1872*, S.O. 1871–72, c. 16. This legislation was substantially modelled after U.K. legislation: *Married Women's Property Act, 1870*, (U.K.) 33 & 34 Vict., c. 93. This parallelism was repeated with the *Married Women's Property Act, 1882*, (U.K.) 45 & 46 Vict., c. 75 and the Ontario statute, *Married Women's Property Act, 1884*, S.O. 1184, c. 19.

1874

The first Canadian local of the Woman's Christian Temperance Union was formed in Picton, Ontario. It was founded by Dr. Letitia Youmans (Armour, p. 15).

1876

The Toronto Women's Literary Club was founded by Dr. Emily Stowe who became the first woman physician licensed to practise medicine in Canada in 1880. The Club was reorganized in 1883 to become the Toronto Women's Suffrage Association (Armour, p. 16).

1885

The *Electoral Franchise Act*, 48–49 Vict., c. 40 defined a "person" who may vote in federal elections as "a male person, including an Indian but excluding persons of the Chinese or Mongolian race." (s. 2) Thus, some men and all women were explicitly excluded from voting.

The *Dominion Elections Act*, R.S.C. 1906, c. 6, s. 67 later provided that "no woman, lunatic, or criminal shall vote." The right to vote in municipal elections was granted to single women and widows in Ontario in 1884: *The Municipal Amendment Act 1884*, 47 Vict., c. 32.

Federal voting power historically derived from the *British North America Act 1867*, 30–31 Vict., (1867), c. 3 (U.K.) which stated that "Dominion elections would be determined in accordance with the provincial franchise until changed by legislation of the Canadian Parliament." In the main, the provincial franchise extended to males possessing substantial property.

In 1898, the *Electoral Franchise Act* was repealed by S.C. c. 14. This restored reliance on the franchises established by the different provinces, effectively eliminated the possibility of aboriginal persons being able to be registered as voters.

1889

The Dominion Women's Enfranchisement Association was formed as an umbrella organization incorporating all suffrage groups in Canada. It changed its name to the Canadian Suffrage Association in 1907 (Armour, p. 22).

1893

The National Council of Jewish Women was formed in 1893.

1894

The National Council of Women of Canada was founded in May 1894.

Its joint purposes have been to serve "the highest good of women, the family and the state." The Council describes itself as bringing women's perspective to the discussion of public policy, and it has the longest history of any Canadian association of presenting an annual brief to the Government of Canada. (Leslie Pearl, "The National Council of Women" (1989) 9 *Jurisfemme* 15.)

Also, in 1894, the Young Women's Christian Association was formed in Montreal.

1897

On February 2, 1897, Clara Brett Martin was called to the Bar in the Province of Ontario and was simultaneously admitted to practice as a solicitor. She became the first woman admitted to the practice of law in the British Empire.

The following material summarises Constance Backhouse's excellent and detailed article, "To Open the Way for Others of My Sex: Clara Brett Martin's Career as Canada's First Woman Lawyer."

Clara Brett Martin*

On 2 February 1897, Clara Brett Martin was called to the bar and admitted as a solicitor in the Province of Ontario. She was the first woman ever admitted to the practice of law in the British Empire. Her struggle for admission was long and difficult; she met and eventually overcame, opposition and insult from classmates, teachers, fellow students at law, Benchers, politicians, and the press.

In 1888, she was admitted to the Arts Programme at Trinity College in Toronto as one of the first women students so admitted. In 1875, Grace Annie Lockhart had been the first woman to graduate from a Canadian University when she received her degree in science from Mount Allison. Clara Brett Martin graduated in 1890 with a B.A. with high honours in Mathematics.

In 1891, she submitted a petition to the Law Society of Upper Canada to permit her to become a student member, a prerequisite to articling as a clerk, attending lectures and sitting the exams required to receive a certificate of fitness to practice as a solicitor. Her petition was rejected by the Law Society after contentious debate, with the Special Committee reviewing the petition interpreting the statute which incorporated the Law Society as permitting only men to be admitted to the practice of law. If such a state of affairs were deemed undesirable, resort should be had to the legislature, the Chair of the Committee noted, since "the function was legislative." Undeterred, or perhaps taking him at his word, Clara Brett Martin succeeded in having her case raised in the Ontario legislature. W.D. Balfour sponsored a bill that provided that the word "person" in the Law Society's statute should be construed to include females as well as males. With the support of the Premier, Oliver Mowatt, legislation in permissive rather than mandatory wording was ultimately passed on 13 April 1892 and permitted the admission of women as solicitors. (*An Act to Provide for the Admission of Women to the Study and Practice of Law*, 1892, 55 Vict., c. 32 (Ont.).)

Initially, the Law Society refused to frame regulations for the admission of women to practice as solicitors as permitted by the legislation. It was deemed "inexpedient" to do so. Premier Mowatt, an Honourary Bencher as Attorney General, subsequently made a motion to the Society that rules be framed to permit the admission of women as solicitors. The vote on the motion was 12 in favour to 11 against. After various unsuccessful machinations, the rules for admission of women as solicitors were presented and approved at a Law Society meeting on 27 December 1892.

The next step for Clara Brett Martin was to register as a student-at-law with the Benchers of the Law Society, which she did on 26 June 1893. Her three years of articling and law society lectures were less than pleasant, being dogged with various degrees of scrutiny, harassment and ridicule. Part way through her articling term, however, she decided that she wanted to be admitted as a barrister as well as a

---

* T. Brettel Dawson. Summarized from Constance Backhouse, "To Open the Way for Others of My Sex: Clara Brett Martin's Career as Canada's First Woman Lawyer" (1985) 1 Can. J. of Women and the Law 1.

solicitor, thus joining battle again with the Law Society over her eligibility to be called to the bar.

The matter was raised directly in the legislature and a bill to permit women to be called to the bar was introduced in 1895 by Sir William Wood. After a vote of 61 in favour and 27 opposed the legislation was passed and received Royal Assent on 16 April 1895. (*An Act to Amend the Act to Provide for the Admission of Women to the Study and Practice of Law*, 1895, 58 Vict., c. 27 (Ont.).)

Clara Brett Martin advised the Law Society in the Spring of 1896 that she wanted to be admitted as a Barrister. Again, the Society deemed it "inexpedient" to frame rules for the admission of women, this time as barristers. Again, Sir Oliver Mowat made a motion that rules be framed to permit this and after a vote of 8 to 4 in favour, rules were slowly drawn up and passed on 18 November 1896 with some contention over the dress code for women appearing in court. Clara Brett Martin filed the necessary papers on 4 December 1896 and received her call to the bar on 2 February 1897, being simultaneously admitted as a solicitor.

She described her experience to a reporter for the Buffalo Express in 1896, in the following terms:

> If it were not that I set out to open the way to the bar for others of my sex, I would have

given up the effort long ago. You would not believe how many obstacles I have had to overcome single-handed. I was articled to one of the largest law firms in Toronto, and when I put in my appearance I was looked upon as an interloper, if not a curiosity. The clerks avoided me and made it as unpleasant for me as they possibly could (I dislike to make such a charge against the young gentlemen of Canada), and for a time it looked as if I were doomed to failure through a source with which I had not reckoned.

Clara Brett Martin built a successful law practice concentrating on conveyancing, mortgages, wills and family law. She maintained an active interest in women's issues and in women's rights generally. She remained single. Her health began to decline by 1920 and on 30 October 1923, at the relatively young age of 49, she died of a heart attack.

In 1989, a letter written by Martin, in which she made anti-semitic comments, was found in the archives of the Law Society of Upper Canada, where all of Martin's personal papers were deposited upon her death.

[See further, a series of articles concerning Clara Brett Martin's anti-Semitism in vol. 5, no. 2 issue of the Canadian Journal of Women and the Law (1992).]

· · · ·

The second woman admitted to the practice of law in the British Empire was Ethel Benjamin, a jewish woman who was admitted in New Zealand, on May 11, 1897. In her excellent B.A. thesis, *Ethel Benjamin:*

New Zealand's First Woman Lawyer, Carol Brown detailed Benjamin's life. What follows has been summarized from her thesis.

Ethel Benjamin*

In New Zealand women had been precluded from the practice of law by the *Law Practitioners Act 1882*. Thus, when she enrolled at the University of Otago in 1893, as the first woman admitted to a law programme in New Zealand, Ethel Benjamin was aware that her entry to a professional career was not certain. She did exceptionally well in her studies toward the LL.B. degree and her progress gave support to promoters of legislation to permit women to practice law. Indeed, her progress has been credited with making the *Female Law Practitioners Act 1896* possible at all. The sponsor of this legislation had argued "of what use is the higher education of women, which is one

of the most prominent features of the education system, if they are to be confined solely to the household and nursery?" (George Russell M.P., *N.Z. Parliamentary Debates* [25 June 1896] at 338)

Pending Benjamin's admission to the Bar, the profession engaged in skirmishes about the proper attire for women barristers. Ultimately Benjamin followed the wig and gown dress code of her male colleagues at her admission on May 11, 1897. Benjamin suffered similar exclusions and slights from the Profession as had met Clara Brett Martin. One difference appears to have been the existence of support among her classmates — which may be explained by

---

* T. Brettel Dawson. Summarized from Carol Brown, Ethel Benjamin: New Zealand's First Woman Lawyer, (Department of History, Otago University, 1985) [unpublished].

the small size of her year at the Law School which had only 13 students.

Once admitted, she practised law in Dunedin and after her marriage, in Wellington. In the early days of her practice she advertised her services and predictably incurred the displeasure of the Law Society. She was very active in the Society for the Protection of Women and Children and acted as honorary solicitor for the Society. Interestingly, unlike many prominent women of her time, she did not subsribe to arguments of women's moral purity to support women's involvement in public and political affairs. Economic independence was a more compelling argument to her.

By all accounts, Benjamin was a feisty, outspoken and confident woman. Her own words provide some insight into her view of her place in law:

> in my own mind, I saw that any talent I had lay in that direction, and because, even as a child, I loved the study of law. (Press interview, 1897)

> When I heard that being a woman I could not be admitted to the practise of the law, I was very indignant, and I suppose, being a true daughter of Eve, the fruit, because forbidden, became all the more attractive and desirable, and I grew all the more determined to follow the legal profession. (Press interview, 1897)

[In a letter of protest to the Secretary of the Law society after being omitted from the invitees to a Bar dinner:]

Another interesting point of divergence from contemporary thought in the women's movement, was Benjamin's representation of the liquor industry in its efforts to resist prohibition.

Benjamin moved with her husband to England in 1908, in part to rejoin her family. Although she was not able to practice law without restriction until the *Sex Disqualification (Removal) Act of 1919*, she joined a legal firm in London and continued her legal career. Benjamin died in October 1943, of injuries suffered when the building she was in collapsed during wartime bombing.

> I am exempted from none of the obligations imposed on members of the Profession, and I consider that all privileges extended to them as such, should also be extended to me.... Moreover, I do not think that without protest I should allow a precedent to be established that may affect the rights of other members of my sex who will follow in my footsteps. (1899)

> For centuries women have submitted to the old unjust order of things, but at last they have rebelled, and as Sarah Grand has it: "It is the rebels who extend the boundary of right, little by little narrowing the confines of wrong and crowding it out of existence." (Press interview, 1897)

. . . .

Other provinces in Canada gradually permitted the admission of women:

Manitoba: *An Act to Amend 'An Act to Amend the Law Society Act', S.M. 1912*, c. 32. The first woman was admitted in 1915.

Alberta: *R. v. Cyr* (1917), 3 W.W.R. 849. Alberta was a departure from the general need to extract legislation to permit admission. The Appellate Division of the Supreme Court of Alberta reversed a lower court decision which had vacated a conviction for vagrancy against Cyr made by Alice Jamieson, a police magistrate in Calgary. Cyr argued that Jamieson lacked the capacity to act in the public office of police magistrate because she was a woman, and hence, that the conviction could be of no effect. Mr Justice Stuart gave the judgement of the Court, concluding:

> I therefore think that applying the general principle upon which the common law rests, namely of reason and good sense as applied to new conditions, this Court ought to declare that in this province, and at this time in our presently existing conditions there is at common law no legal disqualification for holding public office in the government of the country arising from any distinction of sex. And in doing this, I am strongly of the opinion that we are returning to the more liberal and enlightened view of the Middle Ages in England and passing over the narrower and more hardened view, which possibly by the middle of the nineteenth century, had gained the ascendancy in England. (at 858–859)

Saskatchewan: *Legal Profession Act*, R.S.S. 1900, c. 104, as amended S.S. 1912–1913, c. 46, s. 27. The first woman was admitted in 1917.

Nova Scotia: *An Act to Amend Chap. 164, R.S. 1900 'The Barristers and Solicitors Act'*, S.N.S. 1917, c. 41, s. 2. The first woman was admitted in 1918.

Prince Edward Island: *An Act to Amend an Act to Incorporate a Law Society and Amending Act*, S.P.E.I., 1918, c. 14, s. 6. The first woman was admitted in 1926.

Newfoundland: Although not a province of Canada until 1949, the province had formally permitted the admission of women in 1910. *An Act* to Amend Chap. 54 of the Consolidated Statutes (Second Series), entitled, 'Of the Law Society, Barristers and Solicitors,' S. Nfld 1910, c. 16, s. 1. The first woman was admitted in 1933.

Thus, by 1926, all provinces except Quebec (1941) had permitted the admission of women to the practice of law.

[For a full list of the women first admitted for each province in Canada, see C. Harvey, "Women in Law in Canada" (1970–71) 4 Man. L.J. 9.]

During the 1950s, only 4 per cent of those enrolled in Ontario law schools were women. By the 1980s, women comprised 50 per cent of law school students. In 1972, women comprised only 3 per cent of the legal profession in Ontario. In 1991, 20 per cent of practising lawyers were women (*Crossing the Bar*, pp. 26–27).

1900

The Coloured Women's Club of Montreal was formed as a social club and was formally founded in 1902. It aimed to assist black people in Montreal. The club initiated a number of relief and benevolent services, providing warm clothing for newly arrived families (especially immigrants from the Caribbean), introducing them to the existing black community, and suggesting strategies to deal with discrimination. Beginning with the influenza epidemic of 1919, the club maintained a bed in the Grace Dart Hospital. It operated soup kitchens for the unemployed during the 1930s Depression, sent its members to care for the homes and children of hospitalized parents, and provided a plot of land in the Mount Royal Cemetery for the interment of members of the black community whose relatives could not afford burial. The club also provided bursaries for black students. It also worked closely with other black agencies such as, Union Church, the Universal Negro Improvement Association (U.N.I.A.) and the Negro Community Centre. In Ontario, the Eureka Friendly Club was formed in the early 1900s. (Braithwaite, p. 59; Leo Bertley, *Canada and Its People of African Descent* [Toronto: Bilongo, 1977], pp. 293–294.)

1907

The Federation National Saint-Jean Baptiste, the first women's organization in Quebec, was founded by Marie Gerin-Lajoie. Its focus was on improving the working conditions of salesgirls. Under pressure from the Roman Catholic church, the group abandoned its support of suffrage by 1920 (Armour, p. 48).

1908

The Canadian Nurses Association was founded in 1908 (Armour, p. 33).

1910

The Women's Labor League, dedicated to women's suffrage, was formed in Winnipeg in 1910 (Vickers, p. 19).

1912

Mabel French gained the distinction of being the first woman to win the right of admission to the practice of law in two provinces: New Brunswick 1906 (*An Act to Remove the Disability of Women so far as Relates to the Study and Practice of Law*, S.N.B. 1905–07, c. 5) and British Columbia 1912 (*An Act to Remove* the Disability of Women so far as Relates to the Study and Practice of Law, S.B.C. 1912, c. 18). In February 1912, after concerted efforts on the part of a number of women activists, legislation was passed permitting women to become lawyers. Mabel French was admitted on April 1, 1912: according to Watts [History of the Legal Profession in British Columbia 1869–1984], the Benchers' minutes of that date record the call of twenty gentlemen, including Ms. French! (Mary Jane Mossman, "Feminism and Legal Method: the Difference it Makes" (1986) 3 Aust. J. Law and Soc. 30 at n.7.)

1916

Non-aboriginal women were given the right to vote in provincial elections in three provinces:

Manitoba: *An Act to Amend the 'The Manitoba Election Act,'* 6 Geo. V, c. 36

Alberta: *The Equal Suffrage Statutory Law Amendment Act*, 6 Geo. V, c. 5

Saskatchewan: *An Act to amend The Statute Law*, 6 Geo. V, c. 37, s. 1.

. . . .

Emily Murphy was appointed as the first woman police magistrate in the British Empire. Her initial jurisdiction was limited to the City of Edmonton, but later was extended throughout Alberta. She presided over a women's police court. In the extract below, the genesis of the court and of her appointment is outlined together with comment on the operation of the court.

Emily Murphy: Crusader*

On a spring morning, early in 1916, a routine case was tried in the Edmonton court....

About twenty girls had been arrested in a police round-up, charged with being common prostitutes and night-walkers, contrary to section 238, clause (i) of the Criminal Code....

Rumour had it that stool pigeons had been used to gain evidence, and that the women had been given intoxicants prior to their arrest. Later, these rumours were proven to be false, but, at the time, some members of the Local Council of Women felt it was a matter that should be checked. Two delegates from the Law Committee of the Local Council of Women were asked to attend the case in the Guard-room of the Royal North-West Mounted Police, to hear the evidence and to make sure that the women were treated fairly.

With the exception of the girl prisoner who was in the dock...they were the only women in the room.

Seeing them, Counsel for the Crown asked the magistrate to request the women to withdraw from the Court, as the cases were unfit to be heard in a mixed audience.

The women stated that they came as representatives of a committee on laws pertaining to the protection of women and children, and wished to remain.

Counsel replied tartly that decent women, such as they appeared to be, could have no desire to hear the evidence in these cases.

Disconcerted, angry, the women withdrew, as the threat of not being "ladies" was one they could not face. Out in the hall, they telephoned the one woman whom, they knew, would give them sound advice.

Mrs. Murphy's telephone rang. The story was told her, and one of the women asked, "Should we return to court?"

Emily was on definite ground. "Agree with the magistrate," said she. "Such cases should not be heard by a mixed audience. And apply immediately to the government, urging that a court be established for the City of Edmonton in which women offenders may be tried by a woman in the presence of women!"

The women stayed away from the court; but, as always, they insisted that Emily be the one to apply to the Government urging a woman's court.

For several days she shirked the task, and then, without the solace that comes from even one companion, she tackled the Honourable the Attorney-General, Mr. C.W. Cross.

To her amazement, no argument was required. Mr. Cross agreed immediately that such a court was urgently needed.

Then he said, bluntly:

"When are you ready to be sworn in, Mrs. Murphy? The Governor-in-Council meets next week, and your appointment as Police Magistrate will doubtless be ratified."

Shortly after, Emily Murphy was sworn in as Police Magistrate in and for the City of Edmonton. Within a year

---

* Byrne Hope Sanders, *Emily Murphy: Crusader* (Toronto, ON: Macmillan of Canada, 1945) at 131–133, 135, 152, 154 (edited).

she received her commission as Police Magistrate in and for the Province of Alberta.

She was the first woman in the British Empire to be appointed as a police magistrate.

. . . .

As a woman magistrate Emily was fully conscious of the latent power in women's organizations. She was closely allied, throughout this period, with many of them, and worked indefatigably for their interests, drafting resolutions for sponsorship, and programmes of work for development. She felt that if the great women's organizations only cared enough they could bring about the reforms she saw were so desperately needed. Rehabilitation, for instance, was surely women's work. So, too, was the introduction of such national programmes as the payment of wages to male

persons in jail — to be paid for the maintenance of their families. If the prisoner had no family, she believed the wages should be held until he was released. Why should the city or municipality be obliged to support a prisoner's family while the Government got the results from his labour?

. . . .

Encouraged by Emily, many women came to sit in the court and learn what reforms were needed. Hearing the cases without embarrassment, as no men were allowed in, they gained a knowledge of the provisions of the Criminal Code, the Provincial Statutes, the City by-laws. They also learned what was happening in the cabarets, dance-halls, opium dens, cheap lodging-houses, and on the streets, and so were able to take definite action whenever required.

1917

Ontario and British Columbia extend to non-Aboriginal women the right to vote in provincial elections:

Ontario: *The Ontario Franchise Act*, 1917, 7 Geo. V, c. 5; Women, however, could not be elected to the Legislative Assembly, nor could they hold office until 1919: *Women's Assembly Qualification Act, 1919*, 9 Geo. V, c. 8.

British Columbia: *Provincial Elections Act Amendment Act, 1917*, 7–8 Geo. V, c. 23.

The federal *Wartimes Election Act, 1917* S.C. 1917 c. 39, granted the franchise to "qualified women." Of this legislation, Agnes Macphail, Canada's first woman M.P., said in 1929:

I am astounded that [credit should be claimed] for the Conservative party for giving the franchise to women. I do not know of anything more scandalous except the *War Time Elections Act*, of which it was a part, than the manner of granting the franchise to women in 1917. Does the hon. member...and his party not know that it was the starvation and the fighting and the going to jail and the forcible feeding suffered by the suffragettes of Great

Britain, and to a lesser extent of the United States, that gave the franchise to Canadian women?

[At which point some hon. members laughed. Agnes Macphail continued:]

Hon. members do not show good sense in laughing at that. It is true; it is not a thing to be laughed at. The Conservative government...gave votes to women in 1917, but not to all women. That would be too risky...they gave votes to women who they thought would vote for them at that particular time...they gave votes to some women, not to all women, and not because they were intelligent, but because they had a husband or a brother or a son fighting at the front. Whether war time or not, it was a very stupid way of extending the franchise to women. (Hansard, 19 March 1929)

Clearly, during this period, the issue of "votes for women" was a major political and legal issue. The following is an overview of the development of women's access to the vote and related issues.

The Development of Women's Access to the Vote and Related Issues*

A number of women played a leading role in the Canadian suffrage movement, most notably, Nellie McClung, Emily Murphy, Alice Jamieson, Louise McKinney, Irene Parlby and Emily Stowe. The majority

of women who led the movement had relatively high social positions; many were professionals such as doctors, authors and educators and 60 per cent of the female suffragists held jobs. Carol Bacchi has noted

---

* T. Brettel Dawson. Prepared with the assistance of Jennifer Quaile.

that this is a "rather exceptional number" given that in 1911, only 14 per cent of women in Canada were in paid employment.[1] Although innocuously entitled the Toronto Women's Literary Club, this group organized around suffrage in 1876 and seven years later renamed itself the Toronto Women's Suffrage Association. By 1889, the Dominion Women's Enfranchisement Association (later known as the Canadian Suffrage Association) was founded and served as an "umbrella organization" for suffrage groups in Canada.[2] Many existing women's groups also supported enfranchisement, such as the National Council of Women.

Labour groups and organized farm women groups in the Western provinces also actively worked towards the enfranchisement of women through their own organizations; however, few ever joined the ranks of the suffrage societies. Bacchi has suggested that political differences between the organized suffrage movement and the labour and farm women prevented them from working together.[3] The enduring struggle of labour and farm women must not be underemphasized. After all, non-Aboriginal women in three of the prairie provinces were the first to win the franchise.

A turning point for the suffrage movement was the First World War. With an upcoming election, the federal government granted the franchise in 1917 to those women who were British subjects and had a "close relative serving in the armed forces of Canada or Great Britain."[4] The *Wartimes Elections Act, 1917* S.C. 1917, c. 39 was not in any way a victory for the suffrage movement. Its intention was merely to allow men fighting the war overseas to have a sort of "proxy" vote. Cleverdon has quoted the Secretary of State as noting that their female relatives were "likely to vote in such a way...as they themselves would do upon our shores."[5] See also Agnes McPhail's comments on this legislation, as earlier quoted.

The war added fuel to the suffrage movement by demonstrating the work of women on farms and factories in Canada during the war and their service to their country.[6] During discussions in the House of Commons on the Act that would enfranchise women in 1918, the prime minister commented, however, that he was not basing the decision to grant women the vote on "the wonderful and conspicuous service and sacrifice which women have rendered to the national cause in the war" but rather that women were entitled to it "on their merits."[7]

The suffrage movement in Quebec had a tougher battle on their hands to win the provincial franchise. There were two major suffrage organizations. Idola Saint Jean led one group, L'alliance pour le vote des femmes du Québec, which was largely made up of members of the working class with a few teachers and intellectuals. The other group, organized by Thérèse Casgrain, was La ligue des droits de la femme which was a group of middle-class women. These groups arranged to have a woman suffrage bill introduced in the Quebec legislature nearly every year after 1922 for a total of 14 times before the franchise was finally granted to women in 1940. Quebec suffragists ran up against strong opposition from the Roman Catholic Church. In March 1940, Cardinal Villeneuve listed four reasons why women should not vote: (1) suffrage would militate against the family unit; (2) women would be exposed to the passions of elections; (3) most women in Quebec did not want the vote; and (4) social reforms could be achieved by women's organizations outside of politics.[8]

Following 1920, suffrage legislation continued to discriminate on the basis of race and ethnicity. A new provision was added to the Dominion Franchise Bill of 1920 which read:

> Persons who, by the laws of any province of Canada, are disqualified from voting (for) a member of the Legislative Assembly of such province in respect of race, shall not be qualified to vote in such province under the provisions of this act.[9]

Until 1948, Canadians of Chinese, Japanese, and East Indian ethnic origins were not allowed to vote unless they were war veterans. Legislation also prevented Inuit (called Eskimos at the time) from voting until 1950. In British Columbia, all "references to race" were finally removed from legislation in 1953.[10]

---

[1] Carol Bacchi, "Divided Allegiances: The Response of Farm and Labour Women to Suffrage" in Linda Kealy, ed., *A Not Unreasonable Claim, 1880–1920s* (Toronto: The Women's Press, 1974) 89 at 91.

[2] Jill Vickers, Pauline Rankin and Christine Appelle, *Politics as if Women Mattered: A Political Analysis of the National Action Committee on the Status of Women* (Toronto: University of Toronto Press, 1993) at 19.

[3] Bacchi, *supra*, note 3 at 90.

[4] Catherine L. Cleverdon, *The Woman Suffrage Movement in Canada* (Toronto: University of Toronto Press, 1974) at 124.

[5] Ibid. at 125.

[6] Ibid. at 134.

[7] Ibid. at 131.

[8] Ibid. at 257.

[9] Joseph F. Krauter and Morris Davis, *Minority Canadians: Ethnic Groups* (Toronto: Methuen, 1978) at 75.

[10] Ronald Manzer, *Canada: A Socio-political Report* (Toronto: McGraw-Hill Ryerson, 1974) at 280.

In 1924, the federal government awarded the franchise to approximately 4,000 native Indians who were war veterans.[11] The situation with respect to suffrage or enfranchisement for the aboriginal peoples of Canada, including aboriginal women, followed a tortuous route before the unrestricted right to the federal vote established in 1960. The *Indian Act* (1876), 39 Vict., c. 18 provided in s. 3(12) that "the term 'person' means an individual other than an Indian, unless the context clearly requires another construction." The *Electoral Franchise Act* (1885), although including (status) Indians within its definition of "person" went on to exclude from the right to vote "Indians in Manitoba, British Columbia, Keewatin and the Northwest Territories, and any Indian on any reserve elsewhere in Canada who is not in possession and occupation of a separate and distinct tract of land in such reserve and whose improvements on such separate tract are not of the value of at least one hundred and fifty dollars." This limitation was repeated in the *Electoral Franchise Act* of 1890, 53 Vict., c. 8.

In 1898, the *Electoral Franchise Act* was repealed by S.C. c. 14. This restored reliance on the franchises established by the different provinces, effectively eliminating the possibility of aboriginal persons being able to be registered as voters. It should also be noted that at this time, to become enfranchised an Indian man would have to renounce his Indian status, a point repeated in the *Indian Act*, S.C. 1956, c. 40, s. 27. In 1917, the *Military Voters Act*, S.C. 1917, c. 35 extended the federal vote to all Canadian men and women on active duty, including Indians. A similar piece of legislation gave the vote to wives and female representatives of men overseas: *War Times Elections Act* S.C. 1917, c. 39. The *Dominion Elections Act 1920*, S.C. 1920, c. 46, s. 29(1) gave the vote to "Indians who served in the World War (later extended to the Second World War as well) but excluded Indians ordinarily resident on an Indian reservation."

The federal franchise was extended without restriction to aboriginal men and women in Canada in a particularly oblique fashion in 1960 through dual legislative amendments. The *Act to Amend the Canada Elections Act*, S.C. 1960, c. 7 repealed earlier sections of the Act which disqualified all Indians ordinarily resident on a reserve, except those with the military veteran's qualification or unless a waiver from tax exemption had been signed. The *Act to Amend the Indian Act*, S.C. 1960, c. 8 repealed s. 86(2) of that Act which had made it possible for Indians to waive

their tax exempt status in order to vote. The provincial franchise was altered individually by the provinces. Some of the dates of provincial enfranchisement were:

British Columbia: 1949 — S.B.C. 1949, c. 19

Ontario: 1954 — S.O. 1954, c. 25

Manitoba: 1952 — S.M. 1952, c. 18

Saskatchewan: 1960 — S.S. 1960, c. 45

New Brunswick and Prince Edward Island: 1963

Quebec: 1969

The federal vote, then, was not granted to all Aboriginal persons living on reserves until 1960, and they were not granted the provincial vote in Quebec until 1969. A rather optimistic statement given in the House of Commons by the prime minister was that giving the vote to native Indians would mean that "colour or race" would not place "any citizen in our country in a lower category than the other citizens of our country."[12] This sentiment, expressed in 1960, was in sharp contrast to remarks made on 2 May 1885, by one Mr Fairbanks M.P., who made the following statement:

> to give the franchise to women would interfere with their proper position...would be a burden instead of a benefit to them. This, I believe to be exactly the case as regards the Indians. What idea has an Indian of our Government, or of our constitution? How is it possible for the Indian to understand our system of government so that he may be able to exercise in an intelligent manner the right to vote? I do not want to depreciate the intelligence of the Indian, but we must treat him as we find him. The Indian is in an exceptional position, and while he remains in that position, a ward of the government, it will be doing him an injury rather than a benefit to give him a power which neither by training, education nor instinct he is able to appreciate and to wisely exercise.[13]

Although restrictions on the right to vote have been removed in Canada, discrimination remains in some countries. For example, women do not have the franchise in Kuwait, and in Egypt while voting is compulsory for men, women are registered only "on request."[14] Some cantons in Switzerland were resisting the idea of women voting as recently as 1990.

---

[11] Krauter and Davis, *supra*, note 9 at 15.

[12] House of Commons, Debates, Third Session — 24th Parliament 8–9 Elizabeth II, vol. I, at 67 (18 January 1960).

[13] Quoted in Richard Bartlett, "Citizens Minus: Indians and the Right to Vote" (1879–80) 44 Sask. Law Rev. 163, at 173.

[14] Guy S. Goodwin-Gill, *Free and Fair Elections: International Law and Practice* (Geneva: Inter-Parliamentary Union 1994) at 46.

The first country to grant the national franchise to women was New Zealand in 1893.

One of the leading suffragists was Nellie McClung. The extract that follows is from her 1915 book, *In Times Like These*.

In Times Like These*

"HARDY PERENNIALS!"

If prejudices belonged to the vegetable world they would be described under the general heading of: "Hardy Perennials; will grow in any soil, and bloom without ceasing; requiring no cultivation; will do better when left alone...."

Custom and conventionality recommend many and varied occupations for women, social functions intermixed with kindly deeds of charity, embroidering altar cloths, making strong and durable garments for the poor, visiting the sick, comforting the sad, all of which women have faithfully done, but while they have been doing these things, they have been wondering about the underlying causes of poverty, sadness and sin.

. . . . .

Now politics simply means public affairs — yours and mine, everybody's — and to say that politics are too corrupt for women is a weak and foolish statement for any man to make. Any man who is actively engaged in politics, and declares that politics are too corrupt for women, admits one of two things, either that he is a party to this corruption, or that he is unable to prevent it — and in either case something should be done.

If politics are too corrupt for women, they are too corrupt for men; for men and women are one — indissolubly joined together for good or ill. Many men have tried to put all their religion and virtue in their wife's name, but it does not work very well. When social conditions are corrupt women cannot escape by shutting their eyes, and taking no interest. It would be far better to give them a chance to clean them up.

There is another hardy perennial that constantly lifts its head above the earth, persistently refusing to be ploughed under, and that is that if women were ever given a chance to participate in outside affairs, that family quarrels would result.... Father and son have been known to live under the same roof and vote differently, and yet live! Not only to live, but live peaceably! If a husband and wife are going to quarrel they will find a cause for dispute easily enough, and will not be compelled to wait for election day.

What a strange commentary on marriage that it should disqualify a woman from voting. Why should marriage disqualify a woman? Men have been known to vote for years after they were dead!

Quite different from the "family jar" theory, another reason is advanced against married women voting — it is said that they would all vote with their husbands, and that the married man's vote would thereby be doubled. We believe it is eminently right and proper that husband and wife should vote the same way, and in that case no one would be able to tell whether the wife was voting with the husband or the husband voting with the wife. Neither would it matter. If giving the franchise to women did nothing more than double the married man's vote it would do a splendid thing for the country, for the married man is the best voter we have; generally speaking, he is a man of family and property — surely if we can depend on anyone we can depend upon him, and if by giving his wife a vote we can double his — we have done something to offset the irresponsible transient vote of the man who has no interest in the community.

There is another sturdy prejudice that blooms everywhere in all climates, and that is that women would not vote if they had the privilege; and this is many times used as a crushing argument against woman suffrage. But why worry? If women do not use it, then surely there is no harm done; but those who use the argument seem to imply that a vote unused is a very dangerous thing to leave lying around, and will probably spoil and blow up. In support of this statement instances are cited of women letting their vote lie idle and unimproved in elections for school trustee and alderman. Of course, the percentage of men voting in these contests was quite small, too, but no person finds fault with that.

Then, of course, on the other hand there are those who claim that women would vote too much — that they would vote not wisely but too well; that they would take up voting as a life work to the exclusion of husband, home and children. There seems to be considerable misapprehension on the subject of voting. It is really a simple and perfectly innocent performance, quickly over, and with no bad after-effects.

In spite of the testimony of many reputable women that they have been able to vote and get the dinner on one and the same day, there still exists a strong belief that the whole household machinery goes out of order when a woman goes to vote. No person denies a woman the right to go to church, and yet the church service takes a great

---

* Nellie McClung, *In Times Like These* (Toronto: University of Toronto Press, 1972) at 43–45, 47–53, 55–58. Reprinted by permission of University of Toronto Press.

deal more time than voting. People even concede to women the right to go shopping, or visiting a friend, or an occasional concert. But the wife and mother, with her God-given, sacred trust of molding the young life of our land, must never dream of going round the corner to vote. "Who will mind the baby?" cried one of public men, in great agony of spirit, "when the mother goes to vote?"

One woman replied that she thought she could get the person that minded it when she went to pay her taxes — which seemed to be a fairly reasonable proposition.

Another shoot of this hardy shrub of prejudice is that women are too good to mingle in everyday life — they are too sweet and too frail — that women are angels. If women are angels we should try to get them into public life as soon as possible, for there is a great shortage of angels there just at present, if all we hear is true.

Then there is the pedestal theory — that women are away up on a pedestal, and down below, looking up at them with deep adoration, are men, their willing slaves. Sitting up on a pedestal does not appeal very strongly to a healthy woman — and, besides, if a woman has been on a pedestal for any length of time, it must be very hard to have to come down and cut the wood.

These tender-hearted and chivalrous gentlemen who tell you of their adoration for women, cannot bear to think of women occupying public positions. Their tender hearts shrink from the idea of women lawyers or women police-men, or even women preachers; these positions would "rub the bloom off the peach," to use their own eloquent words. They cannot bear, they say, to see women leaving the sacred precincts of home — and yet their offices are scrubbed by women who do their work while other people sleep — poor women who leave the sacred precincts of home to earn enough to keep the breath of life in them, who carry their scrub-pails home, through the deserted streets, long after the cars have stopped running. They are exposed to cold, to hunger, to insult — poor souls — is there any pity felt for them? Not that we have heard of. The tender-hearted ones can bear this with equanimity. It is the thought of women getting into comfortable and well-paid positions which wrings their manly hearts.

Another aspect of the case is that women can do more with their indirect influence than by the ballot; though just why they cannot do better still with both does not appear to be very plain. The ballot is a straight-forward dignified way of making your desire or choice felt. There are some things which are not pleasant to talk about, but would be delightful to vote against. Instead of having to beg, and coax, and entreat, and beseech, and denounce as women have had to do all down the centuries, in regard to the evil things which threaten to destroy their homes and those whom they love, what a glorious thing it would be if women could go out and vote against these things. It seems like a straightforward and easy way of expressing one's opinion.

Then there is the problem of the foreign woman's vote. Many people fear that the granting of woman suffrage would greatly increase the unintelligent vote, because the foreign women would then have the franchise, and in our blind egotism we class our foreign people as ignorant people, if they do not know our ways and our language. They may know many other languages, but if they have not yet mastered ours they are poor, ignorant foreigners. We An-glo-Saxon people have a decided sense of our own supe-riority, and we feel sure that our skin is exactly the right color, and we people from Huron and Bruce feel sure that we were born in the right place, too. So we naturally look down upon those who happen to be of a different race and tongue than our own.

It is a sad feature of humanity that we are disposed to hate what we do not understand; we naturally suspect and distrust where we do not know.

There are people who tell us that the reason women must never be allowed to vote is because they do not want to vote, the inference being that women are never given anything that they do not want. It sounds so chivalrous and protective and high-minded. But women have always got things that they did not want. Women do not want the liquor business, but they have it; women do not want less pay for the same work as men, but they get it. Women did not want the present war, but they have it. The fact of women's preference has never been taken very seriously, but it serves here just as well as anything else. Even the opponents of woman suffrage will admit that some women want to vote, but they say they are a very small minority, and "not our best women." That is a classification which is rather difficult of proof and of no importance anyway. It does not matter whether it is the best, or second best, or the worst who are asking for a share in citizenship; voting is not based on morality, but on humanity. No man votes because he is one of our best men. He votes because he is of the male sex, and over twenty-one years of age.

After one has listened to all these arguments and has contracted clergyman's sore throat talking back, it is real relief to meet the people who say flatly and without reason: "You can't have it — no — I won't argue — but inasmuch as I can prevent it — you will never vote! So there!" The men who meet the question like this are so easy to classify.

I remember when I was a little girl back on the farm in the Souris Valley, I used to water the cattle on Saturday mornings, drawing the water in an icy bucket with a windlass from a fairly deep well. We had one old white ox, called Mike, a patriarchal-looking old sinner, who never had enough, and who always had to be watered first. Usually I gave him what I thought he should have and then took him back to the stable and watered the others. But one day I was feeling real strong, and I resolved to give Mike all he could drink, even if it took every drop of water in the well. I must admit that I cherished a secret hope that he would kill himself drinking. I will not set down here in cold figures how many pails of water Mike drank — but I remember. At last he could not drink another drop, and stood shivering beside the trough, blowing the last mouthful out of his mouth like a bad child. I waited to see if he would die, or at least turn away and give the others a chance. The thirsty cattle came crowding around him, but old Mike, so full I am sure he felt he would never drink another drop of water again as long as he lived, deliberately and with difficulty put his two front feet over the trough and kept all the other cattle away.... Years afterwards I had the pleasure of being present when a delegation waited upon the Government of one of the provinces of Canada, and presented many reasons for extending the franchise to women. One member of the Government arose and spoke for all his colleagues. He said in substance: "You can't have it — so long as I have anything to do with the affairs of this province — you shall not have it!"

Did your brain ever give a queer little twist, and suddenly you were conscious that the present mental process had taken place before. If you have ever had it, you will know what I mean, and if you haven't I cannot make you understand. I had that feeling then...I said to myself: "Where have I seen that face before?" ... Then, suddenly, I remembered, and in my heart I cried out: "Mike! — old friend, Mike! Dead these many years! Your bones lie buried under the fertile soil of the Souris Valley, but your soul goes marching on! Mike, old friend, I see you again — both feet in the trough!"

1917

Helen Gregory MacGill, who had been the first woman to graduate in Arts from Trinity College, University of Toronto in 1889, was appointed as Judge of the Juvenile Court in Vancouver 1917. Also, in 1917, Louise McKinney and Roberta MacAdams became the first women elected to a provincial legislature (Alberta).

1918

An Act to Confer the Electoral Franchise upon Women, 8–9 Geo. V, c. 20 gave non-Aboriginal women the right to vote in federal elections.

. . . .

The first woman to serve as a cabinet minister in the British Empire was Mary Ellen Smith. Smith was elected to the legislature of British Columbia on January 24, 1918, and became a "Minister without Portfolio" on March 24, 1921. See further, C. Cleverdon, *The Women's Suffrage Movement in Canada*.

1919

The Federated Women's Institutes of Canada was founded in 1919. Also, the Canadian Federation of University Women in the same year (Armour, p. 47).

. . . .

In December, the Women's Law Association of Ontario was founded as a professional association. Margaret Hyndman, Q.C. recalled in an interview with Constance Backhouse on June 24, 1984, that although the Association provided an excellent channel of communication for women lawyers, it also was the reason for their subsequent exclusion from the Lawyer's Club.

"When they formed the Lawyer's Club in Toronto in the 1930s, they didn't include women. They said, 'You have the Women's Law Association.' That was a bitter blow." As quoted in Constance Backhouse, "To Open the Way for Others of My Sex: Clara Brett Martin's Career as Canada's First Woman Lawyer" (1985) 1 Canadian Journal of Women and the Law 1 at n.194.

1920

Women were granted the right to hold political office and to sit in Parliament. (Women in New Brunswick became eligible to run for office in 1934.) The first woman to sit in the federal parliament was Agnes Macphail in 1921. Agnes Macphail was a strong advocate for prison reform, old age pensions and abrogation of the legal rule by which a woman who married a non-Canadian lost her nationality. She proposed that the government establish as "Department of Peace" having dual functions: the general supervision of an extensive programme for peace throughout Canada and the cultivation of "friendly relations with other countries by promoting our knowledge of other people with regard to their cultural, moral and social achieve-ments." (1928) She was also one of the greatest orators in Canadian politics.

[See further, Doris Pennington, *Agnes Macphail: Reformer* (Toronto: Simon and Pierre, 1989).]

1924

Vera Parsons became the first woman criminal lawyer in Ontario, and the first woman lawyer to appear before judge and jury. She was also one of the first women lawyers with a disability (She had polio and used a cane.) (*Crossing the Bar*, p. 19).

1928

The Women's Liberal Federation of Canada was formed to attract women to the Liberal Party (Armour, p. 54).

1928–29

The question of whether women are included in the term "persons" eligible to be called to sit as senators was raised in a petition presented by prominent feminists to the government of the day. The matter was referred for decision by the Supreme Court of Canada.

In 1928, the Supreme Court of Canada ruled that women were not among the "qualified persons" eligible to be called to sit as senators: *In the Matter of a Reference as to the meaning of the word 'Persons' in section 24 of the British North America Act, 1867,* [1928] S.C.R. 276.

In 1929, the Judicial Committee of the Privy Council in London, England, overruled the Supreme Court decision, pronouncing that women were indeed "legal persons": *Edwards* v. *A.G. for Canada* [1930], A.C. 124.

A Red-letter Day in the Red Chamber*

Now that Senate reform is once again receiving top billing, it's interesting to note that it was 60 years ago today that the first woman was admitted to membership in what had been Canada's most exclusive male club, the Senate.

Cairine Wilson was a wealthy Ottawa matron who spoke French and was devoted to good works and the interests of the Liberal Party. The daughter of Robert Mackay, a Liberal Senator, and the wife of Norman Wilson, once a Liberal MP, she was appointed to Canada's upper house by an old family friend, that wily bachelor prime minister, William Lyon Mackenzie King.

Her elevation to the Senate on February 15, 1930, took place almost four months after the judicial ruling that made her appointment possible: the landmark decision of the Judicial Committee of the Imperial Privy Council that women were "persons" and therefore eligible to sit in the Senate.

Today we find it difficult to imagine that learned counsels would be asked to debate the meaning of the phrase "qualified persons" as found in Section 24 of the British North America Act. Yet this happened back in the 1920s when Judge Emily Murphy of Edmonton and four other Alberta feminists set out to prove that the reference to "qualified persons" applies to men and women alike.

The disputed section reads: "The Governor-General shall from time to time, in the Queen's name, by instrument under the Great Seal of Canada, summon qualified persons to the Senate; and, subject to the provisions of this Act, every person so summoned shall become and be a member of the Senate and a Senator."

Only the masculine pronoun is employed in Section 23 to describe a Senator's qualifications, so the question was: did Section 24's "qualified persons" include women?

The so-called "persons case" came before the Supreme Court of Canada in 1928, more than six years after Agnes Macphail had become the first woman to sit in the House of Commons and after years of agitation by Canadian women to have a member of their sex appointed to the Senate.

An aroused Emily Murphy instigated the Supreme Court proceedings when, in 1927, she found four other

---

* Valerie Knowles, "A Red-letter Day in the Red Chamber," *The [Toronto] Globe and Mail* (15 February 1990) A7. Reprinted by permission of author.

well-known Alberta feminists — Nellie McClung, Louise McKinney, Henrietta Muir Edwards and Irene Parlby — to join her in petitioning the government for an order-in-council directing the court to rule on the controversial phrase "qualified persons."

Fortunately for the petitioners, Mackenzie King's government was prepared to grant their request. In fact, it considered the subject so important that it defrayed all legal expenses associated with it. The document was forwarded to Ottawa, where, in March 1928, the case came before the highest appeal court in the land and, after weeks of deliberation, all five Supreme Court judges ruled that women were not eligible for Senate appointment.

The judgment was a great blow to the five activists, but it was not enough to knock them out of the fight. When, a year later, the government had not acted on its promise to amend the BNA Act, the determined Albertans appealed to His Majesty's Privy Council in London. [On] October 18, 1929, Lord Sankey delivered the famous judgment reversing the Supreme Court decision.

Never one to rush, Mackenzie King waited until mid-February the following year before making his trial-blazing appointment. However, his choice for Canada's first woman Senator was acclaimed across the country. Mrs. Wilson was widely regarded as the "very antithesis of the short-haired woman reformer," according to The Ottawa Journal. The mother of eight, she was a shy person who shunned the limelight but was an indefatigable worker who had given generously of her time and money to a wide variety of philanthropic organizations.

Mrs. Wilson had also worked hard for the Liberals, having been the driving force behind the establishment of the National Federation of Liberal Women of Canada and the main architect of the Twentieth Century Liberal Association of Canada (an organization for young people).

Although the appointment was lauded, there was some criticism. Many Westerners, for example, thought Emily Murphy or one of the other feminists involved in the original case should have been appointed.

Equally critical were MPs who resented the fact that another male bastion was being invaded by women. And then there were those self-righteous observers who claimed that no wife and mother, let alone one with eight children, should take on the role of Senator.

Militant feminists may have resented Mackenzie King's choice, but it proved to be an excellent one. A hard-working Senator with the courage of her convictions, Mrs. Wilson had a career of great distinction. In the process she even distanced herself from the values of her class and other Canadian elites by publicly denouncing the Munich Agreement in 1938 and by working tirelessly on behalf of refugees, many of whom were Jews fleeing Nazi Germany.

The 12 women who sit in the Red Chamber today owe Cairine Wilson a debt of gratitude for the example she set.

1930

The Canadian Federation of Business and Professional Women's Clubs was founded in 1930 (Armour, p. 55).

1931

Amendments to the Civil Code of Quebec: *An Act to Amend the Civil Code and the Code of Civil Procedure Respecting the Civil Rights of Women*, 21 Geo. V, c. 101 was passed, following the recommendations of the Dorion Commission. Implemented immediately were: control by the wife over her earnings and damages for injury (art. 1425a); free disposal of moveable property by women married in separation (art. 1422); full legal capacity for women separate as to bed and board (art. 210); and increased facility for obtaining separation of property (art. 1311, 1312, 1313, 1314c, 1314d. repealed) (Altschul and Carron).

1934

Helen Kinnear became the first woman in the British Commonwealth to be appointed as K.C. (King's Counsel — an honour granted to senior, respected members of the legal profession).

1937

The *Criminal Code of Canada*, R.S.C. 1927, c. 36, s. 207(a) prohibited the manufacturing, sale, advertisement, distribution, circulation, etc. of "any obscene book or other printed...matter or other object tending to corrupt morals...." By virtue of s. 207(c), it was a criminal offence to offer to sell, or to advertise or have for sale or disposal "any means or instruction or any medicine, drug or article intended or represented as a means of preventing conception or of causing abortion or miscarriage...." If the accused could prove that the public good was served by the acts alleged to have been done, this would constitute a defence pursuant to s. 207(2). One's motive was irrelevant (s. 207(4)).

In 1937, Dorethea Palmer, who worked for the Parents Information Bureau of Kitchener, was charged under s. 207(c) for distributing to women, door-to-door, a pamphlet in English and French, entitled "Birth Control and Some of its Simplest Methods." In addition to distributing the pamphlet, Palmer would discuss the correct use of various types of contraception and assist women to arrange to receive a supply of contraceptive aids from the Bureau. The main issue at her trial was whether her actions "served the public good."

The magistrate's reasoning, in dismissing the charge, makes an interesting study.

R. v. Palmer*

I therefore hold that the acts alleged to have been done by Miss Palmer were done knowingly, without lawful justification, and for the purpose of aiding the Parents Information Bureau to advertise means or instructions intended or represented as a means of preventing conception.

The accused has therefore cast upon her the onus of proving that the public good was served by the acts alleged to have been done and that there was no excess beyond what the public good required.

. . . .

The Criminal Code does not prohibit the use of contraceptive devices. What Miss Palmer is charged with is the advertising of certain means of contraceptives. The broad question of whether the use of contraceptives is or is not for the public good is not for this Court to decide. What the Court has to decide is whether Miss Palmer in advertising contraceptives was acting for the public good and whether there was any excess in her acts.

When one examines the conditions in the Town of Eastview, where over 1,000 out of a population of 4,000 are on relief, where the Province of Ontario has to provide $125,000 out of an annual total of $130,000 relief bill, it is reasonable to assume that in this Town of Eastview there is a large pauper population.

It is a well-known fact that the rich and middle class people who can afford to go to a doctor, can and do obtain information on how to practice contraception and do use these means. It is also true that any person can go to a drugstore and purchase, without any red tape or restriction any number of contraceptive devices. The one class of society from whom this information is being withheld are the poor classes. An examination of birth statistics reveals that the poorer classes are generally breeding large families. Any person who has had any experience with Social Service work or Court work knows of countless poor families where children appear at regular year apart intervals. The mothers are in poor health, pregnant 9 months out of every year. Several witnesses in this case had 9 or 10 children and were aged 30 to 35 years, husband on relief or on small salaries. What chance have these children to be properly fed, clothed and educated? They are a burden on the taxpayer. They crowd the Juvenile Court. They glut the competitive labour market. They are reared in conditions which impair their health. What argument is there from a humanitarian point of view, from the point of view of the public good of humanity that will deny to these people the knowledge and the means of properly spacing these children so that the mother and the child can enjoy good health, and so that parents can control the number of children to the number that they can support in a manner above the mere level of starvation subsistence? And what means are available to these poor families in Eastview to obtain this knowledge? There is no Birth Control Clinic, in Ottawa or Eastview. There are only two doctors in Eastview, both Roman Catholics. The evidence appears to be that the only method of contraceptive that Roman Catholic doctors are permitted to advise is partial continence or the abstention of intercourse during certain periods. It has been pointed out that the majority of women are irregular in their menstrual period and that this method depends upon the time of the period to come. It seems to me that this method, even with the most careful and intelligent application is open to the charge of unreliability. How can one then expect it to be efficacious among the poorer classes where intelligence is often below the general level. The uncertainties of this method surely must have a psychiatric effect upon women that is to say the least undesirable.

Therefore what valid argument can there be against giving these women the most reliable information that medical science has discovered to date?

The pessary, condom and jelly have all been declared by the medical witnesses in this case to be harmless and even to be advised in some cases for therapeutic reasons. There is no evidence to support the contention that they will cause sterility, cancer or infection. It is argued that they will, but there are no experiments, no evidence to support that contention. Rather the evidence tends to contradict this argument. From the evidence I am satisfied that

* *R. v. Palmer* (1937), 68 C.C.C. 20 at 26, 27–29, 31.

these three contraceptives are not harmful. And these three contraceptives are the ones Miss Palmer advertised.

It is argued that as these women are mostly Roman Catholics and that as Eastview's population is 71% Roman Catholic, and as the Roman Catholic Church forbids the use of mechanical and chemical contraceptives that therefore it is not for the public good, for Miss Palmer to advertise to such people. I cannot see the harm of giving scientific truth and knowledge to the people. What they do with that knowledge is their own affair. If their religion forbids it and they accept the tenets of their religion, they will not use the knowledge. But the evidence of some of the witnesses, Roman Catholics, is that they wanted this information and intended to use it, the tenets of their religion notwithstanding. They were women to whom this information would be valuable. Is it for the public good to withhold this information from them?

· · · ·

If therefore there are strong grounds for the dissemination of Birth Control information in Eastview, if there are no other means of Eastview women obtaining this information, if the methods advertised are harmless, if the women witnesses wanted this information and thought there

was nothing wrong in obtaining it and if Miss Palmer, a nurse, had a *bona fide* motive in her work, should not any Court of Law in an honest effort to interpret the law for the well-being of the community come to the conclusion that Miss Palmer's acts were for the public good and that the excess in one or two cases was so small compared to the good in other cases as to amount to no excess at all.

That is the conclusion I have come to, well knowing that opinion is sharply divided on so contentious a question. The development of public opinion in this matter during the past 10 years has been tremendous. Religious bodies even are declaring, in guarded tones, in favour. Social welfare organizations have declared themselves in favour. In Australia 50 years ago, in the case of *Ex p. Collins* (1888), 9 N.S.W.L.R. 497, Mr. Justice Windeyer expressed opinions wholly in accord with mine as outlined above. Is Canada 50 years later still to be wandering in the intellectual and social wilderness on this vital subject?

For the reasons stated above I hold that Miss Palmer has proved that the public good was served by the acts she is alleged to have done and that there was no excess in the acts alleged beyond what the public good required. The charge therefore will be dismissed.

In thinking about the significance of this case, the complexity of movements for social change and the idea of "progressivity," note that the founder of the Kitchener Bureau was A.R. Kaufman, who was a member of the Eugenics Society of Canada. This Society had emerged in the 1930s as "the political voice of those who hoped to cure all manner of social problems through restricting the reproduction of the 'feeble-minded' and genetically inferior."

[See generally, Dianne Dodd, "Women's Involvement in the Canadian Birth Control Movement of the 1930's: The Hamilton Birth Control Clinic" in *Delivering Motherhood: Maternal Ideologies and Practices in the 19th and 20th Centuries*, eds. Katherine Arnup, Andree Levesque, and Ruth Roach Pierson; Margaret Brennan [asst.] (London and New York: Routledge, 1990) 150 at 152.]

Dodd briefly discusses the Palmer case in the following terms:

The trial of one of the Parent Information Bureau's nurses, Dorethea Palmer, who was charged with disseminating contraceptive information in Eastview (now Vanier), Ontario, served as the movement's platform for arguing the benefits of birth control. The defence presented birth control as a technological solution to social, economic and political problems ranging from infant and maternal mortality to poverty, juvenile delinquency and racial ten-

sion, and thus won Palmer's acquittal on the basis of the "for the public good" clause. At the trial, it was only the women, Palmer herself and several middle-class birth control reformers, who stressed the right of women to control their childbearing function, while the male "experts" — economists, sociologists, psychiatrists and social workers — stressed the social, economic and eugenic benefits of birth control....

The Palmer acquittal gave birth-control advocates the legal assurances they needed to carry on their work with reasonable freedom from judicial interference. In Hamilton...public health nurses were forbidden to discuss birth control with clients until 1937, when the municipality began to pass on to the birth-control clinic the names of people who relief officials felt needed birth control. (Dodd, *supra*, at 152 and 154)

Dodd notes that, after the trial, Palmer was quickly dismissed by Kaufman, due to some doubts about her "character" and marital status. (at note 86)

[See also, Dianne Dodd, "The Birth Control Movement on Trial 1936–37" (1983) at 16, 32 Histoire Sociale/Social History 411–428; Angus McLaren and Arlene Tigar McLaren, *The Bedroom and the State: The Changing Practices and Politics of Contraception and Abortion in Canada 1880–1980* (Toronto: McClelland and Stewart, 1986).]

1938

Margaret Hyndman, who had been admitted to practice law in 1926, became only the second King's Counsel in the British Empire. She was the first woman to sit on the board of a trust company (1945), London and Western. She died in 1991. She practised law for 64 years, 30 of them legally blind. In her words, "The only battle that women lawyers needed to win was won in 1897 when Clara Brett Martin won the right to become a lawyer" (MacLaren, at 281).

1940

Women in Quebec did not receive the right to vote in provincial elections until 1940: *An Act granting to women the right to vote and be eligible as candidates*, 4 Geo. VI, c. 7. The right to vote in local elections was delayed until 1941: *An Act to amend the Cities and Towns Act*, 5 Geo. VI, c. 41; and *An Act to amend the Municipal Code*, 5 Geo. VI, c. 69. 1918.

1941

Quebec permitted the admission of women to the practice of law in 1941: *An Act respecting the Bar*, 5 Geo. VI, c. 56 (S.Q. 1941, c. 56, s. 1). Elizabeth Monk and Suzanne Filion were the first women admitted (1942).

1943

Helen Kinnear was appointed as County Court Judge. She was the first woman lawyer in the British Empire to be appointed to a superior court judgeship. The first woman to be appointed as judge in Quebec's Superior Court was Rejane Laberge-Colas, who was appointed in 1969. She was also the founder and first president of the Quebec Federation of Women.

1944

On August 15, the federal government enacted *The Family Allowances Act*, S.C. 1944–45, c. 40, as amended S.C. 1946, c. 50; S.C. 1949, c. 17.

1946

A provision of the *Naturalisation Act, 1914*, 4–5 Geo.V, c. 44, under which women marrying non-Canadians lost their Canadian citizenship, was amended to permit a woman to retain her citizenship if she married a non-Canadian: *Canadian Citizenship Act*, 10 Geo. VI, c. 15.

. . . .

In 1946, Greta Wong Grant became the first Chinese-Canadian lawyer in Canada. This was also the year when Chinese women and children, under the age of 18, were allowed to enter Canada. Chinese men had come to Canada since 1860 to work on the railroad, but Chinese women were not allowed to immigrate to Canada (*Crossing the Bar*, p. 23).

1949

Nancy Hodges became the first woman Parliamentary Speaker in the Commonwealth when she was appointed Speaker in the British Columbia legislature (Armour, p. 66).

1950

The Congress of Canadian Women was founded in 1950 (Vickers, p. 19).

1951

Canadian Negro Women's Association was founded in 1957 (Vickers, p. 19).

. . . .

Ontario permitted women to sit as jurors: *The Jurors Amendment Act*, S.O. 1951, c. 41. In 1952, Manitoba followed suit: *An Act to amend the Jury Act*, 16 Geo. VI, c. 37. British Columbia permitted women to sit as jurors in 1964, and P.E.I. did the same in 1966.

Quebec did not permit this to happen until 1976, LQ c. 9, which provided that women were no longer disqualified from serving as jurors in Quebec. However "domestic obligations" still served as grounds for exemption.

Rose v. The Queen*

MARQUIS, J. [Translation]: — The accused has challenged the panel of jurors on the ground that *The Jury Act*, R.S.Q. 1964, c. 26, s. 2 [re-en. 1971 (Que.), c. 15, s. 2] makes ineligible for jury duty persons of the female sex, together with a great number of citizens whose property holdings or rents do not meet certain standards which are allegedly inequitable. In addition, the accused has also challenged the fact that several members of the same family are also ineligible.

He has based his arguments on the *Canadian Bill of Rights*, R.S.C. 1970, App. III, and in particular upon s. 1(a) and (b) thereof which reads as follows:

1. It is hereby recognized and declared that in Canada there have existed and shall continue to exist without discrimination by reason of race, national origin, colour, religion or sex, the following human rights and fundamental freedoms, namely,

(a) the right of the individual to life, liberty, security of the person and enjoyment of property, and the right not to be deprived thereof except by due process of law;
(b) the right of the individual to equality before the law and the protection of the law.

. . . .

The above-mentioned provision in the *Bill of Rights* does not mean that a certain portion of the population must necessarily be eligible to fill a particular role or to perform a special function, merely because such role or function does not deprive such portion of the population of its liberty, equality before the law and the protection of the law.

The accused has alleged that *The Jury Act* is discriminatory, so that an analysis of what is meant by discrimination and of who may be affected by it becomes necessary.

. . . .

The *Canadian Bill of Rights* does not make use of this word, but the accused's motion and the arguments of his counsel rely heavily upon it.

Addressing myself to the accused's argument, I would say that there is no discrimination where a man is called upon to perform a certain function and a woman is required to fill some other role of equal importance but of a different nature. If the various roles played by men and women in society were to be considered discriminatory, we would be forced to the logical conclusion that all the professions would have to contain an equal number of persons of both sexes, and this would apply to judges, teachers, government officials, etc. Can it really be said that this parity should extend to the area of manual labour, involving the heavy work done by street labourers, miners, workers in heavy industry or, in one word, workers involved in all those activities requiring physical strength not available to woman whose charms and energy, nevertheless, are adaptable to other tasks which are often much more important and more useful?

There is no doubt that women are capable of acting as jurors, as the government of Quebec has recognized in a statute which is to come into force when the jury rolls needed to implement it have been properly prepared.

Turning again for the moment to the *Bill of Rights*, reference is made therein to *the right of the individual to life, liberty, security of the person, equality before the law, and the protection of the law*.

In the instant case, however, it would be incorrect to conclude that women are deprived of their liberty and of their equality before the law, simply because they are ineligible to serve as jurors. Such a function does not constitute an essential attribute of a person's liberty or

---

* *Rose v. The Queen* (1972), 19 CRNS 66 (Que. S.C.).

equality before the law; on the other hand, it is an onerous responsibility which, until now, has not been imposed upon women.

. . . .

The fundamental principle upon which a court must proceed is that *all citizens be treated equally before the law*. In the case at bar, the accused has been brought before the Court under the provisions of the *Criminal Code*, s. 554 which sets out the mechanics by which the jury called upon to decide the fate of one of their fellow citizens must be chosen.

It was strenuously argued that women have not yet been called upon to serve as jurors. Fifty years ago, however, they were not entitled to vote and when they finally obtained this right, a great number of them refused to exercise it. With the advance in modern communications and the progress in the sciences, however, society has come to look more and more favourably upon the exceptional qualities possessed by women in the teaching, educational, scientific, social, administrative and commercial fields. Since the magnificent role of wife and mother has been reserved to women for so long, the legislature did not see sit to impose upon her the onerous task of serving on juries, but today, since she has assumed practically all the social responsibilities, she will be capable of serving as a juror as soon as the jury rolls have been prepared for this purpose, thereby enabling the authorities to set the legal process in motion.

. . . .

The accused's suggestion that the array be challenged and that other jurors be called is unacceptable because a jury cannot be empanelled in the absence of enabling legislation, and the array may only be challenged on the grounds set out in s. 558 (538) of the *Code*, i.e., partiality, fraud or wilful misconduct.

The accused in the instant case is subject to the same rules and the same system as all others accused, and is therefore equal in the eyes of the law. The requirements of equality before the law and the protection of the law within the meaning of s. 1(b) of the *Bill of Rights* have therefore been met.

The jurors' finding, moreover, does not depend upon their age, occupation, profession or sex. Furthermore, the integration of women in juries will constitute a valuable addition to the system, rendering it more humane, but will not permit an accused to escape if he is guilty.

I might also add that there will be more charm in our courts, that the arguments conducted therein will perhaps be more restrained, and that the knowledgeability and good judgment possessed by the women will unite harmoniously with the same attributes possessed by the men.

I agree with the accused that the *Criminal Code* applies to the instant case, but it is and will remain in force until repealed, amended or declared inoperative; I would also agree that *The Jury Act* derives its authority from the *Criminal Code* and embodies a mechanism — albeit one fraught with human imperfections, but nevertheless superior to those in many countries — a mechanism permitting the accused to choose those who will judge him from among a great number of his fellow citizens, *in such a way as to be treated equally before the law and to receive the same protection* as all those who are brought before the criminal courts.

This case does not involve a decision concerning the vindication of the rights of women; it does, however, have to do with the *equality of the accused before the law*, with his right to make full answer and defence, and with the presumption of innocence in his favour.

. . . .

In the instant case, there was no evidence of *partiality, fraud or wilful misconduct on the part of the sheriff or his deputies*.

For the reasons given, I would dismiss the accused's motion and *with due impartiality and in the spirit of justice*, I find that *The Jury Act* of Quebec is still in force and is operative by virtue of the provisions of the *Criminal Code*, and has full legal effect.

Motion dismissed.

[Note: In February 1994, the Supreme Court of Canada, granted leave to appeal in a case in which there had been an all-female jury. The accused, who was convicted, claimed that the jury, by virtue of its gender composition, was biased. (*Biddle*)]

. . . .

The Ontario *Female Employees Fair Remuneration Act*, S.O. 1951, c. 26 was passed. This Act was the first legislation to attempt to equalize pay standards for women and men. In 1956, legislation requiring equal pay for women doing "identical or substantially identical work" to men working for the same employer, was passed federally and also in Manitoba. Alberta followed suit in 1957, and New Brunswick, in 1961. Quebec did not enact equal pay legislation until 1975.

. . . .

Charlotte Whitton became the first woman mayor in Canada; in Ottawa. She died in 1975 (Armour, p. 67).

Thérèse Casgrain, became the first woman leader of a political party in Canada (Co-operative Common-wealth Federation), Quebec. She was an upper-class woman, whose father was a Conservative MP and whose husband was a federal Liberal Cabinet Minister. She was a feminist and nationalist. She claimed to be "less obedient than other women in the early feminist movement" and measured her distance from the Roman Catholic church in Quebec. She believed that women needed equality of opportunity in order to participate in the public sphere. Her feminist organization, *Ligue des droits de la femme*, had different goals than those of the Federation National Saint-Jean-Baptiste. The goals were votes for women, access to the professions and equality before the law. She was one of the prominent founding members of the New Democratic Party in 1961. She was appointed as Senator in 1970 (Susan Mann Trofimenkoff, "Thérèse Casgrain and the CCF in Quebec" in Linda Kealey and Joan Sangster, eds. *Beyond the Vote: Canadian Women and Politics* [Toronto: University of Toronto Press, 1989], pp. 139–168).

1954

The double standard regarding adultery was removed from the Quebec Civil Code which had provided that a husband could obtain a separation if the wife committed adultery, but a wife could only obtain a separation if the husband committed adultery and kept his mistress in the matrimonial home. The Dorion Commission had refused to change this, saying that women forgave more easily, and that the sting of public ridicule is more painful for men (Altschul and Carron, citing Casgrain, *Une femme chez les hommes* [1971]).

1957

Ellen Fairclough was the first federal cabinet minister. She was appointed as Secretary of State in 1957.

> Under pressure to appoint a woman to Cabinet following the 1957 election, Prime Minister John Diefenbaker summoned Fairclough and said, "It looks as though I'll have to form my cabinet from amongst my enemies (Fairclough being one of those voting against him at the leadership convention). You can be Secretary of State." Instead of swooning as Diefenbaker had expected, Fairclough was ticked off. As Labour critic, she had hoped for that at least. Snapping, "I'll let you know," she walked out. She did, however, accept the position and later became Minister of Citizenship and Immigration and then, Postmaster General. (MacLaren, p. 102)

1958

Canada became a member of the United Nations Status of Women Commission. Also, the National Council of Women became an observer for the government (Vickers, p. 19).

1960

The Voice of Women was formed with its main goal of working for peace (Vickers, p. 19).

. . . .

The *Bill of Rights*, S.C. 1960, c. 44. was passed as "ordinary" legislation. Section 1 provided:

> **1.** It is hereby recognized and declared that in Canada there have existed and shall continue to exist without discrimination by reason of race, national origin, colour, religion or sex, the following human rights and fundamental freedoms, namely,
>
> (a) the right of the individual to life, liberty, security of the person and enjoyment of property, and the right not to be deprived thereof except by due process of law;
> (b) the right of the individual to equality before the law and the protection of the law;

. . . .

As noted above, the Aboriginal peoples in Canada did not receive the right to vote in Canadian federal elections until 1960, and in Quebec elections until 1969.

[See also Sally M. Weaver, *Making Indian Policy: The Hidden Agenda 1968–1970* (1981); Jack Woodward, *Native Law* (1989) 145 at n.16.]

It is not clear who was the first Black woman to be admitted to the Bar. Some commentators identify Violet King who was reported as having commenced practice in Calgary during the 1950s (Winks, 1971). The more documented case is that of Myrtle Blackwood who was admitted to the Ontario Bar in 1960 (See *Crossing the Bar, supra*).

1961

Planned Parenthood of Canada was founded (Vickers, p. 19).

1963

Judy LaMarsh, became the second woman to be appointed to the Federal Cabinet when she was appointed as Minister of Health and Welfare. She sponsored the *Canada Pension Plan* and the medicare system. In 1965, she became Secretary of State and held that post during the establishment of the Royal Commission on the Status of Women. She encouraged the participation of women in politics. She also "challenged women's groups by calling them the engine that keeps Canadian political parties functioning — the machinery rather than the engineers" (MacLaren, *infra*, at 76).

> She lacked feminine chic, and her parliamentary colleagues never forgave her for that. When asked about the way LaMarsh was treated, one of her former colleagues exclaimed, "Well, can you imagine going to bed with that?!" For women, politics was guerilla warfare. (MacLaren, p. 103)

1964

Amendments to the Civil Code of Quebec:

> Claire Kirkland-Casgrain, Quebec's only woman cabinet minister, was instrumental in amending the Civil Code through *An Act respecting the legal capacity of married women*, S.Q. 1963–64, c. 66: The wife participates with the husband in the moral and material control of the family and its maintenance, as well as the education of the children (art. 174); the wife may be authorized to take up a separate residence when the husband's choice of residence endangers the physical or moral health of the family (art. 175); a married woman has full legal capacity, subject only to those restrictions arising from her matrimonial regime (art. 177); many impediments to her capacity to contract obligations and assume civil responsibility are removed (arts. 3360 and 1011); the wife separate as to property may, to the same extent as her husband, perform civil acts and contract civil obligations (arts. 1422 and 1424) and the wife in community of property has the same rights subject to her husband's consent (arts. 643, 763, 906, 282, 283, 1292, 178, 1297, 182 and 1415) (Altchul and Carron).

. . . .

The Association for Social Knowledge (ASK), a group of gay men and lesbians, was formed in Vancouver, with the goals of education, community organization and reform of criminal laws (Vickers, p. 20).

1966

The Committee for the Equality of Women was established to lobby for the creation of a royal commission on the status of women. This Committee was a coalition of 34 national and regional associations (Vickers, p. 20).

. . . .

Federation des femmes du Quebec (FFQ) was formed in 1966.

1967

Brenda Robertson was the first woman elected to the New Brunswick legislature and the first woman cabinet minister in New Brunswick (Armour, p. 79).

. . . .

The *Royal Commission on the Status of Women* was established in 1967. Florence Bird was appointed as Chair of the Commission. The report of the Commission was tabled in 1970, and it became an important "founding document" in the contemporary women's movement.

Report of the Royal Commission on the Status of Women in Canada*

TERMS OF REFERENCE

...To inquire into and report upon the status of women in Canada, and to recommend what steps might be taken by the Federal Government to ensure for women equal opportunities with men in all aspects of Canadian society, having regard for the distribution of legislative powers under the constitution of Canada, particularly with reference to federal statutes, regulations and policies that concern or affect the rights and activities of women....

CRITERIA AND PRINCIPLES

1. In a dozen succinct words the Universal Declaration of Human Rights has clarified the issue of the rights of women: "All human beings are born free and equal in dignity and rights."
2. Canada is, therefore, committed to a principle that permits no distinction in rights and freedoms between women and men. The principle emphasizes the common status of women and men rather than a separate status for each sex. The stage has been set for a new society equally enjoyed and maintained by both sexes.
3. But practices and attitudes die slowly. As we travelled across the country, we heard of discrimination against women that still flourishes and prejudice that is very much alive. It became abundantly clear that Canada's commitment is far from being realized.
4. We have been asked to inquire into and report upon the status of women in Canada and we have done so in the light of certain principles. A general principle is that *everyone is entitled to the rights and freedoms proclaimed in the Universal Declaration of Human Rights*. We have examined the status of women to learn whether or not they really have these positive rights and freedoms both in principle and in practice....
5. Explicit in the Terms of Reference given us by the Government is our duty to ensure for women equal opportunities with men. We have interpreted this to mean that equality of opportunity for everyone should be the goal of Canadian society. The right to an adequate standard of living is without value to the person who has no means of achieving it. Freedom to choose a career means little if the opportunity to enter some occupations is restricted.
6. Our Terms of Reference also imply that *the full use of human resources is in the national interest.* We have explored the extent to which Canada develops and makes use of the skills and abilities of women.
7. Women and men, having the same rights and freedoms, share the same responsibilities. They should have an equal opportunity to fulfil this obligation. We have, therefore, examined the status of women and made recommendations in the belief that *there should be equality of opportunity to share the responsibilities to society as well as its privileges and prerogatives.*
8. In particular, the Commission adopted four principles: first, that *women should be free to choose whether or not to take employment outside their homes....*
9. The second is that *the care of children is a responsibility to be shared by the mother, the father and society.* Unless this shared responsibility is acknowledged and assumed, women cannot be accorded true equality.
10. The third principle specifically recognizes the childbearing function of women. It is apparent that *society has a responsibility for women because of pregnancy and child-birth, and special treatment related to maternity will always be necessary.*
11. The fourth principle is that *in certain areas women will for an interim period require special treatment to overcome the adverse effects of discriminatory practices.* We consider such measures to be justified in a limited range of circumstances, and we anticipate that they should quickly lead to actual equality which would make their continuance unnecessary. The needs and capacities of women have not always been

---

* Canada, Royal Commission on the Status of Women, *Report* (Ottawa: Information Canada, 1970), vii; xii–xiii; 387–389; 391–393. Source of information from Privy Council Office. Reproduced with the permission of the Ministry of Supply and Services Canada, 1994.

understood. Discrimination against women has in many instances been unintentional and special treatment will no longer be required if a positive effort to remove it is made for a short period.

. . . .

PLAN FOR ACTION

1. In the course of our enquiry, the Commission has been made aware of the many immediate changes which should be made in existing laws and practices, to "ensure for women equal opportunities with men in all aspects of Canadian society." [...] We were also made aware of the social attitudes which cannot be so readily changed. We cannot ignore the larger issues of customs and beliefs which have given rise to discrimination against women in the past, which continue today, and which may impose new forms of injustice in the future. To implement the recommendations in this Report is only a beginning.

2. We conclude that three lines of action are needed. Within an immediate period we hope to see the implementation of our recommendations, which we believe will do much to improve the lives and opportunities of Canadian women. This will be the task of implementation committees working within a limited term. But in our rapidly changing society, new needs will arise. Action that is appropriate today may become obsolete; new approaches may be needed. Moreover there is a need to keep a continuing watch in order that women's rights and freedoms are respected. We propose two other agencies which would be continuing, with a mandate which would develop in accordance with future demands. One would be concerned with the enforcement of existing laws, which protect the rights of women, to ensure that no discrimination occurs in fact or in interpretation of the law. The other would continue the work of this Commission and would be constituted as the principal agency to create a favourable climate for equality of opportunity for the women of Canada....

. . . .

7. ...We recommend that federal, provincial and territorial Human Rights Commissions be set up that would (a) be directly responsible to Parliament, provincial legislatures or territorial councils, (b) have power to investigate the administration of human rights legislation as well as the power to enforce the law by laying charges and prosecuting offenders, (c) include within the organization for a period of seven to 10 years a division dealing specifically with the protection of women's rights, and (d) suggest changes in human rights legislation and promote widespread respect for human rights.

. . . .

17. We recommend that a federal Status of Women Council, directly responsible to Parliament, be established to (a) advise on matters pertaining to women and report annually to Parliament on the progress being made in improving the status of women in Canada, (b) undertake research on matters relevant to the status of women and suggest research topics that can be carried out by governments, private business, universities, and voluntary associations, (c) establish programmes to correct attitudes and prejudices adversely affecting the status of women, and (d) propose legislation, policies and practices to improve the status of women, and (e) systematically consult with women's bureaux or similar provincial organizations, and with voluntary associations particularly concerned with the problems of women.

18. Several provinces now have women's bureaux or similar organizations within their governments. Where they exist, they are an effective means of protecting the special interests of women. Such organizations are needed at the provincial level and should, as we recommended above, co-operate closely with the Status of Women Council. Therefore, we recommend that, where it has not already been done, each province and territory establish a government bureau or similar agency concerned with the status of women which would have sufficient authority and funds to make its work effective.

CONCLUSION

19. Even in the interval since the establishment of this Commission, there have been signs of change in public attitudes toward many of the problems with which we have been concerned. But the pace is not sufficiently rapid, and there is little public awareness of the extent to which an improvement in the status of women is required or of the overall impact on society which such a change would bring. At issue is the opportunity to construct a human society free of a major injustice which has been part of history.

20. The extension of "woman's place" to all areas of society is part of the world-wide process of democratization. What we have recommended deals only with a few pressing and immediate problems. But what we have in mind is a releasing of positive and creative forces to take on still larger human tasks. Men, as well as women, would benefit from a society where roles are less rigidly defined.

21. To set the stage for this better employment of human capacities, equality of opportunity for women is a fundamental first step. The effect of our recommendations is likely to be more far-reaching than any one recommendation would indicate. The total impact will

be considerably greater than the sum of the changes we propose. But the Commissioners are aware that true equality of opportunity for women and men can only result from radical changes in our way of life and in our social organization and probably must go as far as an equal sharing by parents in the care of their children and a complete reorganization of the working world.

22. The nine-to-five working day and full-time employment are neither sacred nor are they guarantees of efficiency. Productive efficiency may indeed have to yield its place as the sole criterion of employment practices. Human values may assume greater importance. Many rigid constraints that are part of today's economic world may be relaxed, to the benefit of all.

23. We may begin to question why banks, the post office, doctors and dentists are available only during the hours when everyone else is at work. Why is employment so rigidly structured that additional education is almost inaccessible? Should not the educational system stress the need to adapt to a changing society rather than to conform to the habits of yesterday? Flexibility may be introduced in many aspects of social organization as a consequence of the need to establish equality for women. Canada can afford to experiment boldly.

24. Women, as they seek equality, must contend with a society conceived and controlled by men. They require a high degree of resolution to disregard present barriers and to attain the positions which best reflect their ability. But existing structures are not sacrosanct: women must be aware that they are entering a world that can be changed. And men, as they recognize women's claim to equality, may welcome an opportunity to examine Canada's institutions in a new light.

25. We have indicated some of the characteristics of the society that could emerge. The magnitude of the changes that must be introduced does not dismay us, but we are dismayed that so much has been left undone. In terms of Canada's commitments and the principles on which a democracy is based, what we recommend is no more than simple justice.

1968

In this year, the federal divorce legislation was passed, permitting easier dissolution of marriage: *Divorce Act,* S.C. 1967–1968 c. 24. This legislation also made a married women's domicile independent from that of her husband, for divorce purposes (s. 6).

At one time, it was necessary for private acts of Parliament to be passed to obtain a divorce or legal separation and monetary support. One example of such legislation, from S.C. 1879, c. 79, was *An Act for the Relief of Eliza Maria Campbell.*

An Act for the Relief of Eliza Maria Campbell*

PREAMBLE

Whereas Robert Campbell, of the Town of Whitby, in the County of Ontario, in the Province of Ontario and Dominion of Canada, merchant, by his petition to Parliament in the Session of 1876 set forth, that on the sixth day of April, in the year of our Lord, one thousand eight hundred and sixty-three, he was lawfully married to Eliza Maria Byrne, at Whitby, in the County of Ontario, in accordance with the rites and ceremonies of the Congregational Church of Canada; that the said marriage was duly authorized by license duly issued; that the said Robert Campbell and Eliza Maria Byrne lived and cohabited together as husband and wife from the date of such marriage up to the twenty-fifth day of August, in the year of our Lord, one thousand eight hundred and seventy-three; that the said Eliza Maria Byrne, although the lawful wife of the said Robert Campbell, did commit adultery with one George Gordon, at various times at the town of Whitby, in the said County of Ontario, in the said Province of Ontario, previous to and during the month of August, in the year of our Lord, one thousand eight hundred and seventy-three, in particular on the twenty-sixth day of August, in the year of our Lord, one thousand eight hundred and seventy-three, in the said town of Whitby; that the said Robert Campbell made discovery of the said adultery on or about the twenty-eighth day of August, in the year of our Lord, one thousand eight hundred and seventy-three; that the said Robert Campbell had, since the discovery of the said adultery so committed as aforesaid, refused to cohabit, and had not since cohabited with his said wife, and had since lived apart from her; that the said Eliza Maria Byrne had, since the discovery of the said adultery, lived at the town of Whitby aforesaid separate and apart from the said Robert Campbell; that the said Robert Campbell, subsequently to the discovery of the said criminality, brought an action for criminal conversation in Her Majesty's Court of Queen's Bench for Ontario, against the

---

* S.C. 1879, c. 79; [Assented to, 15th May, 1879].

said George Gordon, and recovered a verdict in the said action against the said George Gordon for one thousand five hundred dollars, and entered judgment thereon; that the said Robert Campbell and the said Eliza Maria Byrne so living apart as aforesaid, the said Eliza Maria Byrne brought a suit against the said Robert Campbell in Her Majesty's Court of Chancery for Ontario, seeking to recover and obtain an allowance for alimony from the said Robert Campbell, which said suit was defended by the said Robert Campbell on the ground of said adultery herein before mentioned having been committed by the said Eliza Maria Byrne, and on the fifteenth day of September, in the year of our Lord, one thousand eight hundred and seventy-five, the said court did order and declare that the said Bill of Complaint of the said Eliza Maria Byrne be, and the same was thereby, dismissed out of the said court; that the said Robert Campbell was desirous of having the said marriage dissolved, annulled, and put an end to, so that he might be free from the same, and could contract matrimony with any other person or persons with whom it would have been lawful for him to contract matrimony, if the said Robert Campbell and Eliza Maria Byrne had not intermarried; and that there were four children issue of the said marriage; and the said Robert Campbell prayed that the said marriage might be dissolved, annulled, and put an end to, and that the issue of his marriage with the said Eliza Maria Byrne, and also the issue of any such future marriage, might be declared legitimate; And whereas the said Eliza Maria Campbell, by her petition presented during the same session, humbly set forth that she was lawfully married to the said Robert Campbell, in her father's house at Whitby, on the sixth day of April, in the year of our Lord one thousand eight hundred and sixty-three; that on the twenty-fifth day of August, in the year of our Lord one thousand eight hundred and seventy-three, about four months before the birth of the fourth and last child, issue of the said marriage, the said Robert Campbell, without sufficient cause, treacherously deserted her, took away from her their three children, and had since lived and kept the said children apart from her; that on the twenty-fourth day of September, in the year of our Lord one thousand eight hundred and seventy-three, the said Robert Campbell, with force and violence and with two constables, but without warrant, removed her from his house, and had ever since refused to receive her or their youngest child therein; that he had since refused to maintain her or their child, or to furnish them with necessaries according to his means and condition; that he had repeatedly accused her of adultery, and endeavoured to prove her guilty; that she had not been guilty of adultery; that he had petitioned Parliament for the dissolution of his marriage with her; that the said Robert Campbell had treated her with cruelty, and ill-used and insulted her; that there was no prospect of reconciliation; that she, the petitioner, desired to be divorced *à mensâ et thoro*; that there is no court in Ontario by whose decree such divorce can be effected; that

she was without means for her own or for her child or children's support; that the Court of Chancery of Ontario having refused her petition for alimony, she was without means to secure a revision of that judgment, and that she desired to have the care and custody of her youngest child and of her only daughter; and the said Eliza Maria Campbell prayed that the Bill might not be passed without amendments which would make it an Act providing for such a separation between her and the said Robert Campbell as would be effected in England by a decree for "judicial separation," and compelling the said Robert Campbell to make adequate provision for her support and the support of her children, and giving her the care and custody of at least the two youngest of her children; And whereas the evidence produced by the said Robert Campbell did not prove that his wife, the said Eliza Maria Campbell had ever committed adultery with the said George Gordon, or with any other person; And whereas the evidence produced, as well by the petitioner as by the respondent, proved that the said Robert Campbell had treated his wife, the said Maria Campbell, with cruelty; that he deserted her on the twenty-fifth day of August, in the year of our Lord one thousand eight hundred and seventy-three; that he had not since lived or cohabited with her; that he had not made any provision for her support and maintenance and for the support and maintenance of their youngest child; And whereas the Senate, in the Session of 1877, granted the prayer of the said Eliza Maria Campbell for a divorce from bed and board, and passed a Bill for that purpose, with provisions for her support and maintenance and for the support and education of her child; And whereas the said Bill was not passed by the House of Commons, on the ground that sufficient notice had not been given of the said Bill according to the rules of that House; And whereas the said Robert Campbell still refuses to receive his said wife into his domicile or to maintain and support her while living apart from him, and whereas the said Eliza Maria Campbell has by her petition prayed that a new Bill may be passed identical in terms as nearly as may be with the said Bill of 1877; And whereas it is expedient to grant the prayer of the said Eliza Maria Campbell: Therefore Her Majesty, by and with the advice and consent of the Senate and House of Commons of Canada, enacts as follows:

1. From and after the commencement of this Act, the said Eliza Maria Campbell shall be and shall remain separated from the bed and board of her husband, the said Robert Campbell.

2. The separation hereby authorized and provided shall, except as hereinafter provided, have the same force and the same consequences as a judicial separation in England, under a decree for judicial separation pronounced by the proper court there, at the commencement of this Act.

3. The said Robert Campbell shall pay annually to his said wife for her support and maintenance the sum of

five hundred dollars during her separation as aforesaid, in two equal instalments, payable half-yearly, on the last days of May and November in each year.

4. The said Eliza Maria Campbell may, after the commencement of this Act, have the custody and care of one of the children of the said marriage, namely, Francis William Campbell, during her separation as aforesaid.

5. The said Robert Campbell shall pay annually to his wife, the said Eliza Maria Campbell, the sum of two hundred dollars for the support and education of the said child, while she remains in her custody during the separation as aforesaid. The said sum of two hundred dollars shall be payable in equal half-yearly instalments of one hundred dollars, on the last day of May and November in every year during the minority of the said child.

6. If the said Robert Campbell shall neglect or refuse for the space of ten days after the same is due, to pay or cause to be paid into the hands of the said Eliza Maria Campbell or her attorney, lawfully appointed, any one of the said instalments, it shall be lawful for the said Eliza Maria Campbell to apply to a judge of one of the superior courts of Ontario, or to one of the county judges of Ontario, and the said judge is hereby authorized and empowered to grant her application for an order to the said Robert Campbell to pay the instalment or instalments then overdue,

together with the costs of the said application and order, and if he shall disobey the said order, he shall be deemed guilty of a contempt of court.

7. The said Robert Campbell and the said Eliza Maria Campbell may agree that upon the payment of a certain sum of money in hand, or upon the conveyance of a certain amount of property to her for her sole and separate use, the said Robert Campbell shall no longer be liable to pay the half-yearly instalments aforesaid, or any of them; but no such agreement shall have any force or effect until it has been approved by a judge of one of the superior courts of Ontario, whose approval, after hearing the parties, shall be endorsed on the instrument containing the agreement.

8. Before and until the making and approval of an agreement as aforesaid, this Act may be registered in any Registry Office in Ontario; and such registration shall have the same force and effect as the registration of an order or decree of the Court of Chancery, under section forty-four of chapter forty of the Revised Statutes of Ontario.

9. If, and whenever the said Eliza Maria Campbell and Robert Campbell shall become reconciled and cohabit as man and wife, this Act shall thereafter have no further or other operation or effect than a decree for judicial separation would have in England under like circumstances.

1969

Amendments to the *Criminal Code* decriminalized the dissemination of birth control information and permitted legal abortions to be performed under certain conditions, with the approval of a hospital therapeutic abortion committee.

The Rising of the Women*

ABORTION CARAVAN

In April 1970, a call came from the Vancouver Women's Caucus for women across Canada to join a caravan that would travel from Vancouver to Ottawa, there to confront the prime minister: "We consider the government of Canada is in a state of war with the women of Canada. If steps are not taken to implement our demands by Monday, May 11, 1970 at 3:00 pm, we will be forced to respond by declaring war on the Canadian government."

And so they set out from Vancouver, stopping in a dozen towns and cities en route to Ottawa, holding public meetings and swelling their ranks with supporters anxious to add their bodies to the demonstration planned for Parliament Hill. In Kamloops, Edmonton, Regina, Winnipeg,

the Lakehead, Sudbury, and Toronto, activists knew they were coming, from the invitation issued in *The Pedestal*, the only sustained communications link that women's liberation groups had with each other; they greeted them, billetted them, cooked up hot suppers. (Thirty-five years earlier, another generation of women militants had done precisely the same for another on-to-Ottawa trek of insurgents, travelling the same route.) Up and down the streets of downtown, the caravan drove, blaring from a loudspeaker the Judy Collins version of "We Want Our Revolution," while women sang along and distributed literature and talked to people in the streets. They travelled with a coffin, symbolizing the women dead from illegal abortions, and filled it in one town after another with petitions signed by

---

* Myrna Kostash, "The Rising of the Women" (1981), 2:5 *Broadside* at 12–13, 15. Reprinted by permission of author.

thousands and thousands of women demanding the repeal of the abortion laws. "We worked very hard. I'm sure we knocked on every door in the city to get these names. We felt excitement and affection and bravado, waiting for the caravan. For the first time in my life my head and my feelings came together."

They drove into Ottawa with placards pasted on their cars and vans, drove in with women hanging out the windows, shouting and singing — women drove in from the highway who had been too scared to ever drive the highway before — and in the streets women waved V's and clenched fists back at them. Billetted en masse at a church, they hunkered [sic] down for strategy sessions, trying to arrive, by consensus and collective decision-making, at a plan of action for the weekend, while the menfolk who had accompanied them cooked the meals and "did whatever we needed done to carry out our strategy." They decided that, "disguised" as respectable women and armed with forged passes to the House of Commons galleries procured by sympathetic female support staff on Parliament Hill, they would disrupt Parliament by chaining themselves to their seats. Not everyone would go in: the action could provoke arrests and prosecution. No woman should feel compelled to participate and, besides, she could be useful outside, mounting a diversionary demonstration.

This was the first time that political women admitted that they were scared — in SUPA it had been politically "incorrect" to be scared — and that they didn't want to go on this action because they were scared of getting their wrists broken or of being in jail. That was accepted. I was scared and I remembered that I had always refused to go on big anti-war marches because I was scared. I was still scared but this time I felt it was worth it, even if I had to go to jail for two years. I *wanted* to do this.

And so they sent the men out to hardware stores to get chains and locks and themselves scrounged skirts and shoes and make-up from Ottawa women and then were ready.

On Saturday, May 9, over 500 women and their supporters marched to Parliament Hill and demanded unsuccessfully to meet with Trudeau, Munro, and Turner. (Trudeau was "unavailable" as he was preparing for a trip abroad, Munro was in Geneva, and Turner was playing tennis.) Instead they held a rally. Woman after woman stood up to denounce the abortion laws and the bureaucracy calcifying their implementation, to publicize statistics of death and sterility from abortion, to describe their experiences with hospital boards and doctors, to lead in songs and slogans. "Just Society Just for the Rich!" Doris Power of the Just Society Movement in Toronto stood up to speak:

> As you can see, I am pregnant. Under our new "liberalized" abortion laws I applied for a therapeutic abortion at a Toronto hospital.... When I was refused the abortion, the doctor asked if I would obtain an illegal abortion, I replied that many women did. He then said, "Well, take your

rosary and get to Hell out of here." One of the questions low-income women are asked when applying for abortions is, "Will you agree to sterilization?" [...] We, the poor of Canada, are the dirt shoved under the rug of a vicious economy.... What control can we have over our lives if we have no control over our own bodies?

And then, angered and distressed, they all marched to 24 Sussex Drive, some on the first march of their lives, come all the way from Vancouver and Calgary to shout and sing along with the women who had been in the movement for years, all of them sensing they were part of the same historical motion now, class and age and race and experience subsumed within this wave of women united in sisterhood against the regime of the woman-haters and woman-murderers and woman-crushers. "Women-power to the women-people!" They marched their way past the dumb-founded RCMP guards at the prime minister's residence, sat on the lawn for an hour, and marched out, leaving behind the coffin full of petitions, coat hangers, Lysol, and knives.

Monday, May 11. They got dressed that morning in their "disguises," wearing long-sleeved blouses over the chains wrapped around their arms, and strolled over to Parliament Hill, casually going into the galleries in ones and twos, while a large contingent gathered for a demonstration at the steps of the Peace Tower. In the House of Commons, the Honourable gentlemen were discussing the condition of the carpeting in the visitors' elevators.

At a quarter past three I stood up and started making my speech, demanding free abortion. It took the security guard a fair amount of time to reach me so that I was almost finished by the time he got to me. The woman beside me who had been really nervous stood up as he came towards her — one of these great decisions that she had made — and said she wasn't going to let him touch me. She got totally into it. He grabbed me and he pulled me out and I think we reached the door before the next person started. I was shouting all the while. Outside he said, "Well, dear, you've had your little say, haven't you?" It must have taken us three or four minutes to walk down to the main office. By that time bells were ringing and people were screaming and running all over the place. Another guard came in and said, "There's thirty of them in there and they're all chained to their seats!" It dawned on him that I was not a nut; or that if I was a nut then there were a lot of nuts in there with me. He'd obviously taken nuts out of the gallery before but this was different.

As soon as she had been dragged out, the next woman, chained to her seat by the ankle, stood up and shouted the statement about the right to control of her body, and then another woman and another, in this gallery and that gallery, while the guards rushed frantically from one to the other, unable to drag them out until they got hacksaws and pulled them free from the chains. As they chanted, over and over, "free abortion on demand" and "every child a wanted child," the Speaker adjourned the session, the first time in the history of the Canadian House of Commons that it was closed because of a disturbance. The women were photographed by the RCMP but were not arrested. They rejoined their supporters outside and there staged a mock funeral and burned a facsimile of the Criminal Code. Removing their black headscarves, symbolic of the deaths of women by illegal abortions, they revealed red scarves underneath and with fists in the air chanted, "no more women will die." (*Carillon*, 21 May 1970)

On Monday, the same day that women were chaining themselves to their seats in the House of Commons, women in Vancouver, dressed up in bizarre costumes, "witched" the federal courthouse: they glued up onto a wall a declaration that the federal government was killing the women of Canada and splashed it with red paint. A man, charged with being an accomplice to the defacement of federal property, became the women's movement's first official martyr in the courts. (In the end, he got off.)

1970s

Legislation guaranteeing human rights were promulgated in most provinces during this decade. Some of the legislation replaced more limited "civil rights" legislation.

The Ontario *Human Rights Code*, S.O. 1981, c. 53 (as amended) was first enacted in S.O. 1961–62, c. 93. It replaced the *Racial Discrimination Act*, S.O. 1944, c. 51 and the *Ontario Anti-Discrimination Commission Act*, S.O. 1958, c. 70.

1970

Lena Pederson became the first woman member of the Northwest Territories Council (Armour, p 85).

1971

Margaret Birch became the first woman cabinet minister in Ontario (Progressive Conservative Party) (Armour, p. 90).

. . . .

The National Ad Hoc Committee on the Status of Women was formed in 1971 (Vickers, p. 20).

. . . .

Mabel Van Camp became the first woman appointed to the Ontario Supreme Court. Court officials contacted England and Australia for suggestions on the title to give Van Camp and were told by these countries that they would simply follow Canada's lead (*Crossing the Bar*, p. 44).

1972

The "Strategy for Change" conference was held (funded by the federal government) where the National Action Committee on the Status of Women (NAC) was founded by more than 30 pre-existing groups. Its goal: to monitor the implementation of the royal commission's recommendations. By 1982, it had a membership of 230 groups; by 1988, 575 groups (Vickers, p. 20).

. . . .

Rosemary Brown became the first Black woman to be elected to a Canadian legislature when she was elected as a New Democratic Party member for the riding of Vancouver Burrard in the British Columbia legislature. In 1970, she had been appointed the first Ombuds-woman for the Status of Women, and in 1973 she received a National Black Award of Canada, which was presented to her at the first National Black Awards ceremonies held in Toronto. In her address to the Black Women's Congress in 1973, she said:

I learned that this country, this Canada, is beautiful and strong only because of the people of both sexes and of all races and political persuasion who living in it contributed to this culture and its soul and its growth. And that is its strength and its beauty which will increase only to the extent that it is able to accept and respect all of its people equally. (Quoted in Leo Bertley, *Canada and its People of African Descent* [Toronto: Bilongo, 1977] at 308)

In another 1973 address, this time to Women for Political Action she mused:

I have two fears that are centered around the role of women in politics. One, that we might make the same mistake that the suffragists made, and after some token victory retire thinking that we had won the war when really we would have won one battle. The other, that we might find that after having achieved 50 per cent representation in the political arena, that nothing else had changed; that poverty and despair would still be the lot of most of the women of this country, and that the exploitation of people and resources and our environment would still be raging un-checked in a competitive, ruthless society which destroyed all but those most conditioned to cope with it. It is my hope that somehow you and I will be able to ensure that these fears will never be realized.

...Why cannot power be seen as a creative force? Why cannot creative use of resources be power? Why cannot cooperation be seen as power? Why use the term "power" at all? ... It is my belief that politics can be the evolution of a different way in which people relate to each other.... It is crucial that women entering politics today see themselves not as individuals alone, but as members of a con-stituency working for and dedicated to change.

...All of us [have read books] which tell us how to succeed in the male-oriented climb up the ladder to success. We all know the rules. The question is, do we play by those rules? And, if we do, for how long? We must bear in mind that the longer we play by those rules, and the more adept we become at making those rules work for us, the harder it will be for us to decide, or work, to change them (Rosemary Brown, "A New Kind of Power" in *Women in the Canadian Mosaic*, Gwen Matheson, ed. [Toronto: Peter Martin, 1976] at 290, 293, 294, 298. See also, Rosemary Brown, *Being Brown* [1989]).

In 1975, Rosemary Brown became the first woman in Canada to challenge the leadership of a federal political party (NDP). She lost on the third ballot to Ed Broadbent.

1973

Jean Folster was the first Native woman to be appointed as a magistrate in Manitoba (Armour, p. 96).

. . . .

Muriel Fergusson became the first woman Speaker of the Senate. She had been appointed to the Senate in 1953 (Armour, p. 94).

. . . .

The First Canadian lesbian conference was held in Toronto.

. . . .

The Canadian Association for the Repeal of the Abor-tion Laws (CARAL) was formed; renamed as the Canadian Abortion Rights Action League in 1980 (Vickers, p. 20).

. . . .

The Supreme Court of Canada decided two major cases affecting women's rights.

In one, the judges rejected an argument that section 12(1)(b) of the *Indian Act* which provided that Indian women marrying non-Indian men lost their Indian status, constituted sex discrimination and was impermissible under Section 1 of the Bill of Rights. In *Attorney General (Canada)* v. *Lavell*, [1974] S.C.R. 1349, "the Supreme Court stated that the guarantee to 'equality before the law' in the Canadian Bill of Rights, meant only equality in the administration and enforcement of law. The actual substance of the law could discriminate between men and women, as long as the law was applied by its administrators in an even handed manner." (See E. Atcheson, M. Eberts, and E. Symes, *Women and Legal Action* [Ottawa: CACSW, 1984] at 14–15.)

In the second case, the Supreme Court judges refused to recognize that a farm wife had any legal interest in land belonging to her husband, notwithstanding that she had helped work and develop it. Reaction to this decision spurred development of matrimonial property reforms in Canada and elsewhere in the British Commonwealth: *Murdoch* v. *Murdoch*, [1975] 1 S.C.R. 423.

Per Martland J. at 374–375:

> In the present case, the trial judge has made no such finding [that the wife had made a substantial contribution to the farm operations, as held in the *Trueman* case], but was of the

view that what the appellant [wife] had done, while living with the respondent [husband], was the work done by any ranch wife.

In dissent, Laskin J. referred, at p. 380, to the wife's testimony at trial as to what she did:

> Haying, raking, swathing, moving, driving trucks and tractors and teams, quieting horses, taking cattle back and forth to the reserve, dehorning, vaccinating, branding, anything that was to be done. I worked outside with him, just as a man would, anything that was to be done.

. . . .

Advisory councils on the status of women were established by the federal government and by the Quebec government. The Canadian Advisory Council on the Status of Women was established as an independent government-funded organization to conduct and publish research, to promote public awareness and to advise the Minister Responsible for the Status of Women on matters relating to women. The establishment of these bodies, resulted in part from a recommendation of the Royal Commission the Status of Women.

The National Congress of Black Women of Canada was organized in April, at a meeting convened by the Canadian Negro Women's Association. In a speech to the Congress, Rosemary Brown commented, "Because we are black and because we are female, this conference has given us the opportunity to explore the two liberation struggles which we are sitting astride at this moment." The Congress is a non-profit organization which provides a national forum through which black women can voice their concerns.

1974

The Native Women's Association of Canada (NWAC) was incorporated as a non-profit organization. Native Women's Association of Canada's *Profile, Principles, Structure* (updated April 1990) describes the Association in the following ways:

> The NWAC is founded on a collective goal to enhance, promote, and foster the social, economic, cultural, and political well-being of First Nations and Metis women within Aboriginal and Canadian societies....
>
> NWAC is structured according to the Four Directions, which also entrenches our way of governing ourselves. In working toward the accomplishment of our goals, the four universal principles of TRUST, SHARING, STRENGTH, and KINDNESS are inherent in all that we say and do. Everything revolves around ensuring a future home for our children, and for the next seven generations.
>
> The principles or objectives of the Native Women's Association of Canada [include] to: address issues in a manner which appropriately reflects the continuously changing needs of Native women in communities across Can-

ada; to assist and promote common effects toward self-determination and self-sufficiency for native peoples in our role as mother and leaders; to promote equal opportunities for Native women in programs and activities that meet their social, economic, political, spiritual, and cultural needs; to serve as a resource among our Native women's organizations and communities...to be the national voice for Native women...

> The NWAC receives core funding through the Aboriginal Women's Program, administered by the Department of Secretary of State....
>
> For the first fourteen years of NWAC's existence, our structure was similar to most non-governmental organizations. It was a hierarchical system — a system that was based on "power" and the individuals who held that power; it was also a system that is ultimately alien to our concepts of the universe.... At NWAC's 14th Annual General Assembly...we adopted an organizational structure [based on the teachings of the Four Directions].

Since its inception, the Association has been involved in many issues respecting Aboriginal peoples, generally, and Native women and [their] families specifically. In recent years, [the Association] has concentrated on effecting amendments to the Indian Act, attaining guaranteed equality rights in the Canadian Constitution and increasing [their] participation in the movement toward re-establishment of Aboriginal governments.

1975

The National Association of Women and the Law was founded as a "Canadian non-profit feminist organization devoted to research and public education in areas in which the law has a specific impact on women" (NAWL, 1989). The purpose of the organization was stated as being to "promote the equality of women, in law and in society," with additional goals being "to contribute a perspective on legal issues which furthers equality for women, to support women involved in the legal system, to inform the public about legal matters affecting the status of women and to unite people who are committed to improving the legal status of women." (NAWL Constitution, arts. II, IIB).

. . . .

Agnes Sempler of the Northwest Territories was the first Aboriginal woman to be appointed as Justice of Peace.

. . . .

An honorary doctorate of laws degree was conferred on Carrie Best by Saint Francis Xavier University, in recognition for her human rights work among myriad other undertakings. In conferring the degree, the president of the University described Best as "a woman of outstanding worth, a tenacious crusader for good and noble causes, a gracious lady who had devoted her life and her generous gifts to the betterment of the human condition." Leo Bertley reports that in order to have first hand knowledge of the various black communities about which she wrote [in her newspaper, *The Negro Citizen*], Best visited them. "She was able in this manner to test the degree of racial discrimination that existed in public places. This motivated her to urge the formation of a National Association for the Advancement of Coloured People. Fortunately for Nova Scotians, this idea became a reality." In 1973, Best received the first award given by the National Black Coalition of Canada to black people who have contributed to the cause of justice. Best received the Order of Canada in 1974. (Leo Bertley, *Canada and its People of African Descent* [Toronto: Bilongo, 1977], pp. 267–68; Braithwaite, p. 20.)

. . . .

International Women's Year declared by the U.N. in 1975.

. . . .

Canadian Research Institute for the Advancement of Women (CRIAW) was founded in 1975.

. . . .

Grace Hartman became the first woman elected as president of a major national Canadian union, the Canadian Union of Public Employees. She worked at getting collective bargaining rights for working class women. She led an illegal strike of working women and was jailed for it. She was the "first woman" in many national and international union offices. She was chair of the National Action Committee on the Status of Women (NAC), 1974–75; president of CUPE (first woman president) 1975–76; and first woman representative to the Public Service International (in its 75-year history), where she served as vice-president from 1983–85 (Vickers, p. 184). Hartman died in 1993.

Another woman who made significant contributions in this arena was Madeleine Parent, a union leader in Quebec. She worked for 20 years on the NAC executive. As a symbol of the working class women in NAC, she represented the interests of women textile workers in NAC's Employment and Economy Committee concerning the Canada-U.S. free-trade deal. In 1986, she reported on the *Forget Task Force on Unemployment Insurance* and warned that it threatened to cut 15-week maternity benefits. As a result, the government's planned changes were not implemented (Vickers, p. 236).

1976

Rosalie Abella became the first Jewish woman to be appointed as judge in the Ontario Provincial Court. She began her term in the Family Division of the Provincial Court while pregnant (*Crossing the Bar*, p. 1).

1977

The Quebec government included protection from discrimination on the basis of sexual orientation in the provincial Charter of Rights.

. . . .

MATCH, a non-profit, non-governmental development agency, was formed in Ottawa to facilitate the exchange of information among Canadian and Third World women's groups, researchers, academics, development workers and aid recipients (Armour, p. 110).

. . . .

In November, women in Toronto first met to form Women Against Violence Against Women (WAVAW). Its first action was a Take Back the Night March.

WAVAW was active until 1980, and then went into abeyance until a series of sexual assaults occurred in Toronto, in 1986. Women committed to the principles of WAVAW reformed the group and their actions led to the apprehension of the rapist. The group was active in supporting a legal claim of negligence made by one of the women sexually assaulted, against the Metropolitan Toronto Police Force for their handling of the investigation. The police did not warn women in the narrowly defined high risk category, ostensibly because they feared that women would become hysterical. The police argued in a preliminary motion, that legally there could be no cause of action against them. At the first instance they were unsuccessful, and on appeal: (*Jane Doe v. Police Board of Commissioners [Metropolitan Toronto]* 48 C.C.L.T. 105), permitting the case to go to trial.

The original demands of WAVAW were contained in a 1977 provisional statement:

WAVAW: The Way We Were*

STATEMENT OF PERSPECTIVE AND INTENT

WAVAW is women fighting for women. WAVAW's orientation is specifically feminists in content, structure and execution. It is conceived of as but one segment of a broad struggle which women are waging throughout the world. It in no way replaces or supersedes any other feminist struggle or group.

WAVAW believes that violence against women differs fundamentally from violence against men. Much of the violence between men (such as war, fights for the possession of women or other "property") has a traditionally heroic aspect to it which confirms men's position and strength. Other kinds of violence between men, such as racial attacks, get much of their energy from ignorance and fear of the distant and strange. Women's experience of violence is totally different from men's. Violence "happens" to us supposedly as a natural and "normal" consequence of being female. Even if we escape physical violence to our bodies, and that is rare, we can never escape the constant assaults on our psyche which totally dominate the world we live in. This world is deeply misogynistic. Its violence against our deepest selves scars and destroys us. WAVAW intends to fights this violence against women on all fronts.

WAVAW specifically rejects the passive role of victim in which women have been cast and which is continually forced upon us. WAVAW's declared policy and practice is to initiate, encourage, and support strong and positive actions by women against all violence against us. WAVAW totally rejects any so-called "solutions" to the problem of violence against women which perpetuate fear among women and increase reliance on the existing power structures or on male protection generally.

WAVAW's list of demands summarizes our position on major areas of violence against women. WAVAW is open to any women who agree with those demands and with the general perspective expressed in this document.

Any group of women which endorses this statement (including demands) and acts in a manner consistent with

---

* "WAVAW: The Way We Were" (1981) 3:2 *Broadside* at 17. Reprinted by permission of Resources for Feminist Research (RFR), Toronto, Ontario.

it can be considered part of WAVAW and may receive any support or help within the power and resources of the present WAVAW group.

WAVAW may support any women on any one or more issues listed under DEMANDS, whether or not these women support ALL the WAVAW demands, as long as their perspective on the specific issues(s) is feminist and consistent with that of WAVAW.

WAVAW will not actively seek cooperation with non-feminist, non-women-only groups. WAVAW may align itself on any specific issue with any group, organization or individual whose objectives coincide with WAVAW on that issue, or whose position or resources may be helpful in carrying on the struggle or solving a specific problem (e.g. arrest).

WAVAW's intention is to contact as many women and groups as possible for the purpose of building a women's network of communication, cooperation and mutual support. WAVAW is presently compiling a list of women's organizations and groups in the Metro Toronto area. Input is needed from the women's community at large, especially from small, informal units such as consciousness-raising and feminist study groups, women's fitness, self-defence and self-improvement classes, women's art and craft groups and similar.

WAVAW DEMANDS

1. *We insist* on freedom of movement for all women, in any part of the city or country, at any time. *We insist* on our right to remain unmolested physically and verbally wherever we are and whoever we are. *We insist* on our right to defend ourselves and each other by any means available.

2. *We insist* on action which focuses on taking the profit out of violence and hate propaganda wherever it occurs and NOT harassment of working women who have few enough choices as it is. *We insist* that the current hypocritical "cleanup Yonge Street" campaign be stopped. *We insist* that police, who now "serve and protect" business interests which profit from violence and hate, stop harassing lesbians and prostitutes. *We insist* on full civil rights for all women, especially lesbians and visible minorities.

3. *We insist* on the decriminalization of prostitution.

4. *We insist* that rape is a crime based on hate and not on sex. It is an act of violence against the whole person of the woman intended to intimidate and to confirm men's power over all women. *We insist* that the law and the courts treat it as an assault and not a "sexual" crime.

5. *We insist* that police and courts respond to wife and child-beating as they would (or should) to any assault. *We insist* that women cease to be coerced to remain or return to intolerable home situations. *We insist* that all women but especially poor, native and immigrant women, have the means to escape and a place to escape to. *We insist* on adequate support for Nellie's Hostel for Women, Rape Crisis Centre and other places necessary for our safety and survival. *We insist* that these remain under the control and direction of women who staff them and women they serve.

6. *We insist* on the elimination of female job ghettos and the growing wage gap between men and women. *We insist* on full economic self-sufficiency of women.

7. *We insist* on the right of any woman to bear and raise children in dignity and freedom from economic want. *We insist* on adequate support for single mothers and welfare women and on day care for all children who need it and want it. *We insist* that children not be separated from their mothers because of their mothers' lesbianism.

8. *We insist* that abortion be taken out of the Criminal Code. *We insist* on the provision of women-run clinics where good health care, birth-control information, and safe abortions will be available free to all women. *We insist* that the need for back-street abortions be removed.

9. *We insist* on dignified treatment of women in prisons and all so-called correctional institutions. *We insist* on feminist training and good pay for female staff and on non-sexist counselling for all women.

10. *We insist* on the right of women to express themselves sexually and not be harassed or discriminated against for lesbian and sexual orientation. *We insist* that lesbians be covered by the Human Rights Code.

11. *We insist* that forced sterilization of immigrant and native women be stopped.

12. *We insist* on an end to violence against women in mental health institutions and the offices of private psychotherapists. Such violence takes the form of sexist counselling, the abuse of shock treatment, extensive drug therapy and psychosurgery. *We insist* on provision of adequate feminist therapy and referral services.

1978

Nadine Hunt became the first woman to head a provincial labour federation, the Saskatchewan Federation of Labour (Armour, p. 111).

The Lesbian Mothers' Defence Fund was launched in Toronto by a group called Wages Due Lesbians (Vickers, p. 21).

. . . .

1979

The Feminist Party of Canada was founded in Toronto in 1979. Some 700 women attended and supported the organization. The Party estimated that at the current rate of progress, it would take 843 years to achieve equal numbers of men and women MPs (Armour, p. 117).

. . . .

On 18 December, the *Convention on the Elimination of All Forms of Discrimination against Women* (CEDAW) was adopted by the United Nations General Assembly. It entered into force as an international treaty on September 3, 1981, after the twentieth country had ratified it. By 1989, almost 100 nations, including Canada, had agreed to be bound by its provisions. Article 3 of the Convention provides:

State Parties shall take in all fields, in particular in the political, social, economic and cultural fields, all appropriate measures, including legislation, to ensure the full development and advancement of women, for the purpose of guaranteeing them the exercise and enjoyment of human rights and fundamental freedoms on a basis of equality with men.

1980

Jeanne Sauvé was appointed the first woman Speaker of the House of Commons. In 1984, she was installed as Canada's first woman Governor-General. She was first elected as a member of the House of Commons in 1972 and was appointed Minister of State for Science and Technology (1972), Minister of Environment (1974), and Minister of Communications (1975). As Speaker, she established the first day care centre on Parliament Hill (MacLaren, pp. 95, 213).

. . . .

The Canadian Congress of Black Women was founded at the seventh annual conference for black women.

The Canadian Union of Postal Workers (CUPW) ratified the contract that included a non-discrimination clause protecting "gay people" — the first such protection for federal government employees (Vickers, p. 21).

1982

On April 17, the *Canadian Charter of Rights and Freedoms*, was enacted as part of the *Canada Act 1982*, c. 11 (U.K.) [Schedule B]. It came into force in 1982, except for section 15, which contained equality guarantees, and which was subject to a three-year delay. The following is an overview of the process by which the Charter equality guarantees were developed.

The Process to Charter Equality Guarantees*

In 1981, one of the most intense lobby campaigns in the history of the Canadian women's movement occurred. After a series of conferences of first ministers beginning in 1978, the federal government tabled its first draft of the *Canadian Charter of Rights and Freedoms* in the House of Commons in 1980 as part of the Constitutional repatriation package. By the time it was introduced, a relatively small group of women with legal expertise was aware of the Charter's omission of women's rights to equality in law and

---

* T. Brettel Dawson. Prepared with the assistance of Jennifer Quaile.

were "on full alert" to organize and prepare briefs to propose amendments.[1] This group became the nucleus of the Ad Hoc Committee of Women on the Constitution.

The first draft of section 15 (the "Non-discrimination Rights" clause) of the Charter, read:

15.(1) Everyone has the right to equality before the law and to the equal protection of the law without discrimination because of race, national or ethnic origin, colour, religion, age or sex.

(2) The section does not preclude any program or activity that has as its object the amelioration of conditions of disadvantaged persons or groups.[2]

It was evident that section 15(1) would not guarantee women equality if "laws themselves were discriminatory".[3] This had been one of the main problems with the 1960 *Bill of Rights*. Women also wanted the section to be renamed "Equality Rights."

Section 1 guaranteed civil rights "subject only to such reasonable limitations as can be demonstrably justified in a free and democratic society with a parliamentary system of government."[4] Feminist lawyers called this "the Mack truck clause" because of the size of the legal loophole. They recommended that section 1 be rewritten to affirm human rights and to include "an overriding statement of equality between women and men."[5] Section 1 was an important element of the Charter because it guaranteed the rights and freedoms defined in other sections of the Charter albeit subject to "reasonable limitations." This limitation and the manner in which it could be interpreted concerned women's groups which were anxious to ensure that women's right to equality in other sections of the Charter would not be undermined by section 1.

Women's groups also recommended that section 7 guaranteeing legal rights to life, liberty, and security of the person should include protection of reproductive rights.[6] The National Action Committee on the Status of Women (NAC) and the Canadian Advisory Council on the Status of Women (CACSA) presented briefs to the House of Commons again emphasising the importance of "entrenching" women's rights to equality in the Charter.[7]

Women's groups and their recommendations were not always taken seriously during the process of presenting briefs. A comment by the co-chair of the Special Joint Committee on the Constitution of Canada, Senator Harry Hays, is evidence of this: "I want to thank you girls for your presentation.... But I wonder why you don't have anything in here for babies or children. All you girls are going to be working and who's going to look after them?"[8] This comment received attention in the media, however, and may have served to heighten the awareness of Canadian women to the task at hand. Women active in the lobby campaign certainly recognized the effort required to implement their recommendations. They were met with opposition from the Minister Responsible for the Status of Women, Lloyd Axworthy, who cancelled a planned national meeting of CACSW on women and the constitution. This was one of the factors leading to the resignation in January 1981 of then CACSW president, Doris Anderson.

Also in January 1981, the federal government announced revisions to the Charter, which included renaming section 15 "Equality Rights" and rewriting certain phrases such as "equality before the law and under the law" and "equal benefit and protection of the law." These amendments addressed some of women's concerns. A phrase in section 1 which had linked the reasonable limitations "with a parliamentary system of government," was also removed in order to strengthen the review function of courts and to "encourage courts to strike down unconstitutional law."[9] Section 1 still contained no guarantee of equality rights; women insisted that sexual equality be an "absolute rather than subject to the 'reasonable limits' test in section 1."[10]

---

[1] This group included Beverley Baines, Rosemary Billings, Linda Ryan-Nye, Marilou McPhedran, Mary Eberts, Beth Atcheson and Beth Symes. See generally, Sherene Razack, *Canadian Feminism and the Law: The Women's Legal Education and Action Fund and the Pursuit of Equality* (Toronto: Second Story Press, 1991) at 29, 33–34.

[2] Gwen Brodsky and Shelagh Day, *Canadian Charter Equality Rights for Women: One Step Forward or Two Steps Back?* (Ottawa: Canadian Advisory Council on the Status of Women, 1989) at 15.

[3] Ibid. at 15.

[4] Penny Kome, *The Taking of Twenty-Eight: Women Challenge the Constitution* (Toronto: The Women's Press, 1983) at 33.

[5] Ibid. at 33–34.

[6] Ibid. at 35.

[7] The Canadian Charter of Rights and Freedoms is "entrenched," which means that it cannot be changed unilaterally by any province or the federal government. Rather, changes may be made only through constitutional amendment. See Lynn Smith and Eleanor Wachtel, *A Feminist Guide to the Canadian Constitution* (Ottawa: Canadian Advisory Council on the Status of Women, 1992) at 29.

[8] Kome, *supra*, note 4 at 36.

[9] Ibid. at 40.

[10] Ibid. at 40–41.

Through remarkable efforts on the part of a group of about a dozen women who organized other women, a national meeting was organized in a matter of weeks without the support of CACSW.[11] This meeting was held in February 1981 and its first resolution was an endorsement of an "entrenched" Charter.[12] An intense lobby campaign was mounted as a result of this meeting. Women were determined to lobby MPs about women's issues, women's rights and hold regular press conferences to keep the public informed. The Ad Hoc Committee of Women on the Constitution received support from various women's groups across Canada and members of the Committee began to gain "a new respect" from federal politicians.[13]

In March 1981, the Ad Hoc Committee discussed section 28 and agreed to the wording "notwithstanding (ss. 1, 7, 27) anything in this Charter, the rights and freedoms set out in it are guaranteed equally to male and female persons." If they could get acceptance of the wording by the government it would be a major victory for them because they considered section 28 to be the most important section of the Charter. The government announced its support of section 28 in the summer of 1981.

In September 1981, however, the Supreme Court of Canada[14] ruled that there was a constitutional convention requiring substantial agreement among the provinces before the *British North America Act* could be amended in a way that affected provincial powers.[15] With such encouragement from the Supreme Court, some of the provinces embarked on a set of negotiations with the federal government on constitutional changes. The judgement and the negotiation process which ensued, however, threatened to jeopardise the gains that the women had already made. Some provinces claimed that their existing human rights codes were sufficient to ensure equality and a number of provincial officials favoured overriding Section 28. A series of meetings of the provinces and the federal government led to the November Accord in 1981.

An override clause (section 33) was added to the Charter as a result of the "insistence of several provinces."[16] Section 33 read:

> Parliament or the legislature of a province may expressly declare in an Act of Parliament or of the legislature, as the case may be, that the Act or a provision thereof shall operate notwithstanding a provision included in section 2 or sections 7 to 15 of this Charter.

The Prime Minister suggested that section 28 might be overridden with the result that there would be no guarantee of equality between women and men. Indeed, section 28 then read: "Notwithstanding anything in this Charter except section 33, the rights and freedoms referred to in it are guaranteed equally to male and female persons".[17]

The struggle resumed. The women mounted an intense lobby campaign to the provincial premiers. Within one week, they were successful in getting the agreement of six provinces to prevent the use of section 33 to override section 28. The federal government insisted, however, that unanimous consent of the provinces was required. The lobbyists also planned to take their case to the Supreme Court for a determination of the legality of an override clause. As a result of the lobby campaign, the Justice Minister announced that section 28 would be reinstated in its earlier form: "Notwithstanding anything in this Charter, the rights and freedoms referred to in it are guaranteed equally to male and female persons."[18] Members of the Ad Hoc Committee were, of course, relieved but did not rejoice.

Kome quotes one member, Linda Ryan-Nye: "Twenty-eight was a helluva lot to lose.... But it was not a helluva lot to win."[19] Brodsky and Day note that while section 28 was intended to call attention of the courts to women's "long and unfinished struggle for equality" as a group, "unfortunately, on the face of it, section 28 does not articulate the right of women to

---

[11] These women included Kay Macpherson, past-president of NAC; Laura Sabia, past president of several women's organizations' Moira Armour, Linda Ryan-Nye and Margaret Bryce from Women for Political Action; Ada Hill of the Federation of Women Teachers' Associations of Ontario; Shelagh Wilkinson of the *Canadian Women's Studies Journal*; Nancy Jackman; and Janka Seydegart. See Kome, *supra*, note 4 at 43.

[12] Kome, *supra*, note 4 at 59.

[13] Ibid. at 75.

[14] *Reference re Amendment of the Constitution of Canada (Nos. 1, 2, 3) Patriation Reference Case* (1981), [1981] 1 S.C.R. 753, 125 D.L.R. (3d) 1, [1981] 6 W.W.R. 1 at D.L.R. 84.

[15] Smith and Wachtel, *supra*, note 7 at 51.

[16] Ibid. at 51.

[17] *House of Commons Debates, Official Report.* First Session — Thirty-Second Parliament, 30 Elizabeth II, Volume XII (1981), 24 November 1981, at 13174.

[18] Ibid. at 13195.

[19] Kome, *supra*, note 4 at 95.

equality."[20] Rather, it guarantees rights and freedoms equally to men and women.

Sections 15 and 28 were both of crucial interest to women. The final draft of section 15 read:

> 15.(1) Every individual is equal before and under the law and has the right to the equal protection and equal benefit of the law without discrimination and, in particular, without discrimination based on race, national or ethnic origin, colour, religion, sex, age or mental or physical disability.
>
> (2) Subsection (1) does not preclude any law, program or activity that has as its object the amelioration of conditions of disadvantaged individuals or groups including those that are disadvantaged because of race, national or ethnic origin, colour, religion, sex, age or mental or physical disability.[21]

Due to the efforts of women, both sections 15 and 28 provided "a stronger constitutional foundation for equality claims than exists in most parts of the world."[22]

The consequences of the guarantees of equality in the Charter have not been entirely positive for women. While the Legal Education and Action Fund (LEAF) was formed to promote women's equality in the courts, other groups were organized to oppose laws that advantaged women. For example, Men and Women for a Fair Market Wage, whose member groups included the National Citizens' Coalition and R.E.A.L. Women of Canada, was organized under the premise that the pay equity law "violated the holy constitutional principles of supply and demand." A group called In Search of Justice was also formed which opposed all forms of affirmative action and advocated fathers' rights in abortion decisions and rights of those accused of sexual assault.[23]

The results of a study of constitutional equality litigation in Canada during the first three years of the Charter indicate that fewer than 10 per cent of equality rights decisions were made on the basis "that a rule or practice infringes the sex equality guarantee" of the Charter. Furthermore, less than 1 per cent of these decisions were "made by or on behalf of women."[24]

As a result of the successful Charter lobby efforts of women, the Status of Women Cabinet portfolio gained newly found "clout" politicians and the media appeared to be more sensitive to women's issues and the grassroots network of the women's movement was strengthened.[25] Managing to get equality rights entrenched in the Charter can be seen as a major political victory for women in Canada. However, the alleviation of women's subordinate position in society is yet to occur. While women may enjoy formal, legal equality, still substantive inequality remains.

[See also Penny Kome, "Anatomy of a Lobby," *Saturday Night* (January 1983) 9–11; Chaviva Hosek, "How Women Fought for Equality" (1983) Canadian Forum 6.]

. . . .

Wife-battering was considered a joke by Members of the House of Commons:

Debates, House of Commons, May 12, 1982*

Status of Women
Parliamentary Report on Battered Wives — Government Action

Mrs. Margaret Mitchell (Vancouver East): Madam Speaker, I have an upbeat question for the minister responsible for the Status of Women. The minister knows that the parliamentary report on battered wives tabled in the House yesterday. It states that one in ten husbands beat their wives regularly.

Some hon. Members: Oh, Oh!

Mrs. Mitchell: These women —

Some hon. Members: Oh, Oh!

Mrs. Mitchell: I do not think it is very much of a laughing matter, Madam Speaker.

---

[20] Brodsky and Day, *supra*, note 2 at 37.

[21] Smith and Wachtel, *supra*, note 7 at 38.

[22] Ibid. at 38.

[23] Michael Mandel, *The Charter of Rights and the Legalization of Politics in Canada* rev'd ed. (Toronto: Thompson Educational Publishing, 1994) at 379.

[24] Brodsky and Day, *supra* note 2 at 49.

[25] Kome, *supra* note 4 at 98–99.

---

* House of Commons, *House of Commons Debates* at 17334 (12 May 1982). Published by Queen's Printer (HANSARD). Source of Information from Legal Council Office, House of Commons Canada. Reproduced with the permission of the Minister of Supply and Services Canada, 1994.

An hon. Member: I don't beat my wife.

Mrs. Mitchell: Madam Speaker, I do not think it is a laughing matter. I would like to say that the battered wives in these cases rarely have any refuge. They have no safe place to go with their children. Police who are called on an emergency basis rarely respond to domestic calls. Charges are not laid in the courts, and there are very few instances of prosecutions in our judicial system.

- (1440)

I want to ask the minister responsible for the status of women what she intends to do immediately in a major way — we do not want just reports, research and conferences — at the federal level to protect battered women.

Some hon. Members: Hear, hear!

Hon. Judy Erola (Minister of State (Mines)): Madam Speaker, I too am not amused by the derision which greeted the statement that one in ten women is beaten. I do not find that amusing, and neither do the women of Canada.

Some hon. Members: Hear, hear!

Mrs. Erola: The hon. member is quite right in asking what can be done at the federal level. I intend to pursue with my colleague, the Minister of National Health and Welfare, procedures which we think the federal government can take to offer the kind of leadership which will lead to an increase in the number of transition homes. Currently this matter comes under the Canada Assistance Plan, and we will review that program to see how we can open it up to provide some sort of leadership. There certainly are not enough homes in this country. I have taken that up with the people who attended the conference with me during the past day and a half. It is one of the recommendations I intend to pursue.

Mrs. Mitchell: Madam Speaker, I note that the minister is again passing the buck to the provinces and not getting at the federal responsibility.

Debates, House of Commons, May 13, 1982*

Status of Women
Call for Apology by House of Commons — Motion under S.O. 43

Mrs. Margaret Mitchell (Vancouver East): Madam Speaker, I rise under the provisions of Standing Order 43 on a matter of urgent and pressing necessity. I ask for support of this motion by all parties in the House. Yesterday many male members of the House laughed uproariously when they were told that one out of every ten men in Canada beat their wives repeatedly. As a result, there has been a public outcry against the appalling attitude expressed by these hon. members. Therefore I move, seconded by the hon. member for Beaches (Mr. Young):

> That all members of this House apologize to the women of Canada for the shameful and disgusting display of discrimination and ignorance by members who degraded this House yesterday with their performance.

Madam Speaker: Is there unanimous consent for this motion?

Some hon. Members: Agreed.

Some hon. Members: No.

. . . .

[Translation]

Status of Women
Regret Concerning Reported Attitude of Members — Motion under S.O. 43

Mr. Marcel Roy (Laval): Madam Speaker, under the provisions of Standing Order 43, I wish to remind hon. members of an incident that occurred in the House yesterday when a question was being put to the Minister responsible for the Status of Women, the Hon. Judy Erola, and some hon. members seemed to be unmindful of the situation concerning wife battering. I move, seconded by the member for Kingston and the Islands (Miss MacDonald):

> That the House apologize for this attitude and shows that its members are aware of the extent of the problem of violence done to women in Canada, and that it reiterate its support for the third report of the Standing Committee of the House and urge hon. members to support its main objectives, which are to gain a better understanding of the problem of violence and provide better protection for its victims.

Madam Speaker: Is there unanimous consent for this motion?

Some hon. Members: Agreed.

Some hon. Members: No.

---

* House of Commons, *House of Commons Debates* at 17368 (13 May 1982). Published by Queen's Printer (HANSARD). Source of Information from Legal Council Office, House of Commons Canada. Reproduced with the permission of the Minister of Supply and Services Canada, 1994.

Debates, House of Commons, May 14, 1982*

Status of Women
Gravity of Family Violence Issue — Motion under S.O. 43

Mrs. Ursula Appolloni (York South-Weston): Madam Speaker, under the provisions of Standing Order 43 I would like to move, seconded by the hon. member for Don Valley East (Mr. Smith):

That this House assure the women of Canada that the issue of family violence and especially of wife battering, is considered by all members of this House to be an extremely grave and alarming one; and that the Report on Violence in the Family, tabled in this House last Tuesday as a result of deliberations in committee by members from all sides of this House, will be given serious consideration by all members in recognition of the fact that wife battering takes place in every constituency across Canada, and affects one out of every ten women.

Some hon. Members: Hear, hear!

Madam Speaker: Is there unanimous consent for this motion?

Some hon. Members: Agreed.

Madam Speaker: Is the hon. member rising to debate the motion?

Mrs. Appolloni: Yes, Madam Speaker. This subject is far too important to be allowed to drop so easily in the House of Commons. I recommend, first of all, that the report from the committee be recommended reading in every school across Canada so that children will begin to learn from an early age that women are not chattels, that women are being battered, and that up until now society has unfortunately turned a blind eye.

I very much hope that as a result of this report, and of deliberations on all sides of the House, Canadian society will learn to treat women with respect, and will give them the protection they need.

Some hon. Members: Hear, hear!

Hon. James A. McGrath (St. John's East): Madam Speaker, in rising to support this motion I want to say on behalf of my party that we very much regret what happened in the House yesterday, or at least the way in which the incident was reported yesterday, because I do not believe the House intended, yesterday or at any time, to belittle this report or the importance of it.

• (1110)

I want to say we commend the committee for its excellent report. We believe it is a very serious problem in the country, probably more widespread than is generally believed. We feel very strongly that not only should the House address itself to the report in this way, but that the government, through the Minister of Justice (Mr. Chrétien) and the Solicitor General (Mr. Kaplan), should address itself to this report so that the people who are the subject of the report, namely, battered wives, can receive the same protection of the laws of Canada as all other groups.

Mr. Neil Young (Beaches): Madam Speaker, I too join with other members in this House in congratulating the committee for bringing forth such a report, and would urge the government to take immediate action on its implementation.

Madam Speaker: Does the House agree to adopt the motion?

Some hon. Members: Agreed.

Motion agreed to.

MPs Agree Wife-beating Is Alarming**

Ottawa — Members of Parliament, embarrassed by an incident this week that saw several of them laugh at the mention of wife-beating, agreed unanimously yesterday to assure women they consider family violence a "grave and alarming" issue.

Male MPs from both sides of the Commons had guffawed and joked Wednesday when New Democrat Margaret Mitchell referred to a Commons committee report that said one in 10 Canadian women are beaten by their husbands.

One members shouted, "I don't beat my wife."

On Thursday, Mitchell, MP for Vancouver East, urged the Commons to "apologize to the women of Canada for the shameful and disgusting display of discrimination and ignorance."

However, her motion did not receive the necessary unanimous consent, nor did a similar motion from Laval Liberal Marcel Roy, chairman of the committee which issued the report on family violence Tuesday.

---

* House of Commons, *House of Commons Debates* at 17423–424 (14 May 1982). Published by Queen's Printer (HANSARD). Source of Information from Legal Council Office, House of Commons Canada. Reproduced with the permission of the Minister of Supply and Services Canada, 1994.
** Gazette News Service, "MPs Agree Wife-beating Is Alarming," *The [Montreal] Gazette* (15 May 1982), A9. Reprinted by permission of the Gazette, Montreal, Quebec.

Yesterday, MPs, clearly shocked by their response to the issue, agreed unanimously to a motion introduced by Liberal MP Ursula Appolloni that called on members to "assure the women of Canada that the issue of family violence, and especially wife-battering, is considered by all members of this House to be an extremely grave and alarming one."

Appolloni also urged all MPs to give serious consideration to the report "in recognition of the fact that wife-beating takes place in every constituency across Canada."

She moved the motion under Parliamentary rules enabling members to seek unanimous agreement on matters of "urgent and pressing necessity."

Such motions seldom pass and even more rarely engender debate, but Appolloni demanded time to speak, saying the issue was "too important to be dropped so easily."

"I very, very much hope that as a result of this report and of deliberations on all sides of this House that Canadian society will learn to treat women with respect and give them the protection they need," she said.

. . . .

The appointment of the first woman to the Supreme Court of Canada was announced when Madam Justice

Bertha Wilson was appointed to the highest court in Canada from the Ontario Court of Appeal.

Speaking Her Mind:
Supreme Court Judge Bertha Wilson*

Thirty-six years ago, a shy, determined woman politely rejected advice that she abandon her plans to study the law, go home to her husband and take up crocheting. Today, Bertha Wilson sits on the Supreme Court of Canada, where her keen intellect and pointed pen have influenced the lives of millions of Canadians. But few recognize the name; fewer still, the face.

The highest-ranking woman judge in Canada is controversial, yet intensely private. Still, her written pronouncements on legal and social questions and her rare public addresses on policy matters have catapulted her onto the front pages time and again.

Through it all, the most prevalent theme has been her faith in the dignity and supremacy of the individuals who are vulnerable against society.

Because these have often been women, the Scottish-born Wilson, who turns 67 later this month, has been praised as an enlightened feminist and condemned as a racial advocate for women.

History will likely remember her as a humanist. Yet Wilson, who in 1982 became the first woman appointed to Canada's Supreme Court, has a tough, gutsy side. Indeed, Lord Ackner of the British House of Lords knows first hand the strength of her convictions.

Wilson likes to ask foreign judges how many women sit on their superior court. When she put the question to Ackner last year at a conference he confided to her that no woman sat on Britain's high court because none is qualified.

The exchange came during a private meeting that was also attended by Madam Justice Sandra Day O'Connor, who in 1981 was the first woman named to the United States Supreme Court.

Shortly afterward, the three appeared together on a panel. Ackner spoke first, making light of the fact that since he was being followed by two women, he would have to protect his backside.

O'Connor followed and said Ackner had done a commendable job. Not Wilson. She promptly repeated his earlier comment about women judges, causing an embarrassed Ackner to sputter, "That was said in confidence."

Such openness did not come as a surprise to the Canadian lawyers and judges in attendance, who are accustomed to the most liberal-minded judge on the nine-member court speaking her mind.

Wilson stirred up heated debate earlier this year by saying what only someone in her position could say: that some Canadian laws discriminate against women. And she didn't stop there. She also stated quite bluntly that a gender bias exists on the bench.

"A distinctly male perspective" that exists in the law has led to "legal principles that are not fundamentally sound," Wilson said in a speech at Osgoode Hall Law School.

. . . .

Wilson was born Bertha Wernham on September 18, 1923, in Kirkcaldy, Scotland. She attended the University of Aberdeen and after earning a master's degree decided to become a teacher.

But in 1945, the year she graduated at age 21, she married John Wilson, a minister in the Church of Scotland. They moved to a small, rural Scottish village where the new Mrs. Wilson found herself ministress of the manse.

---

* David Vienneau, "Speaking her Mind: Supreme Court Judge Bertha Wilson," *Toronto Star* (13 September 1990) D1, D3. Reprinted with permission — The Toronto Star Syndicate.

Wilson learned about poverty, sickness, helplessness and fear. At the same time, she developed a determination to try to set things right. In later years, this would manifest itself in efforts to curb the undue powers of the state.

"I became intimately involved with the drama of the daily life of these people, their joys, their sorrows, their terrible tragedies," she said in September 1982, while speaking to the Ottawa Women's Canadian Club.

FORMAL EDUCATION

"It was the beginning of my formal education in living and, from where I sit on the bench today, it's just as important to know about people as it is to know about the law."

In 1949, the Wilsons moved to Canada, where John Wilson, now retired, worked as a minister in Renfrew. In 1954, they moved to Halifax, where Wilson decided that, at age 31, she would like to return to school.

It wasn't easy. One law professor, Horace Read, a somewhat cantankerous individual, sneered: "Why would someone like you, at age 31, with a husband to look after you want to study law?"

Wilson replied: "I want to study law as part of a liberal education."

Read barked: "Look, my dear, we have no room here for dilettantes. Why don't you just go home and take up crocheting?"

After graduating in 1957, Wilson worked briefly in Halifax before moving to Toronto, where she became the first woman hired by the prestigious firm of Osler, Hoskin and Harcourt. She also became the first lawyer to head the firm's research department, a pioneering role that has since been adopted by many other large firms.

This meant Wilson, who speaks with a lovely, thick Scottish burr, never actually met with clients. Instead, she read and analyzed judgments and law reports, and wrote opinions for her male colleagues.

She became the firm's first female partner and stayed until 1975, when she became the first woman to be named to the Ontario Court of Appeal.

NEW LEGAL GROUND

In 1980, Wilson broke new legal ground by issuing a ruling that gave the go-ahead to an East Indian woman to sue Seneca College for racial discrimination. The woman, who had a PhD in mathematics, had made 10 applications for teaching jobs but had never been granted an interview.

The Supreme Court later overturned the decision, saying the proper remedy for the woman was the traditional route of applying to the Ontario Human Rights Commission for compensation.

By 1982, Wilson herself was on the Supreme Court.

Cracking one of the oldest men's clubs in Canada was no easy task. With 107 years of masculine tradition, the job was not for the faint of heart.

Her friends say those first few years were incredibly difficult, despite the best efforts of some of her male colleagues to make her feel part of the team. She has since been joined on the court by Claire L'Heureux-Dube and Beverley McLachlin.

As Wilson's confidence grew, so did her workload. She writes more legal opinions than any other member of the court. Between October 1987 and August of this year, for example, she authored 81 opinions, far ahead of Chief Justice Antonio Lamer, second with 58.

"She has exceeded all expectations," says John Whyte, dean of law at Queen's University. "She has made a tremendously zealous effort to make her legal opinions resonate with social experience."

That effort was never more evident than in Wilson's clear and forthright decision on abortion rights in January, 1988, when the Supreme Court ruled 5–2 that the arbitrary nature of the old law violated a woman's constitutional right to security of the person.

In her part of the majority judgment, which was not supported by any of the male judges who participated in the ruling, Wilson said a decision to have an abortion is not just a medical one, but a profound social and ethical one as well.

Simply put, said Wilson, it was something men could never understand.

"It is probably impossible for a man to respond, even imaginatively, to such a dilemma, not just because it is outside the realm of his personal experience, but because he can relate to it only by objectifying it, thereby eliminating the subjective elements of the female psyche, which are at the heart of the dilemma."

It was yet another example of Wilson explaining her decision in the straightforward language of the people. Whenever possible, she avoids legalese.

FACED CRITICISM

As a result, she has been criticized for being too independent and for wading far beyond the traditional way of legal thinking. Some critics say at times she even appears prepared to rewrite the Constitution to suit her own personal opinions.

A study of the first 100 Charter decisions by Morton and Peter Russell, a University of Toronto political scientist, has found that Wilson is by far the most prepared among judges to use the Charter to strike down unfair or discriminatory laws.

She did so in a remarkable 53 per cent of cases, well above the court average of 37 per cent. Russell attributes this in part to her background, which is so unlike that of any other judge.

"She is a very humane person with a deep sense of support for the underdog," he says. "Other judges don't have the life experience she has. When you tend to spend life with the big hitters on Bay St., you don't have that perspective."

Constance Glube was the first woman appointed Chief Justice of a trial division of a provincial Supreme Court, in Nova Scotia (MacLaren, p. 271).

1983

Reforms were enacted to the *Criminal Code* provisions relating to rape law. A new offence of "sexual assault" replaced the old rape provisions. In addition, spousal immunity was removed together with the recent complaint rule.

New provisions were introduced delineating and restricting the circumstances in which the sexual conduct of the complainant with persons other than the accused can be admitted into evidence. These provisions were challenged by some accused men as being contrary to the *Canadian Charter of Rights and Freedoms* and they were struck down by the Supreme Court of Canada in the 1991 case of *Seaboyer* v. *R.*, 1991] 2 S.C.R. 577. Bill C-49, *An Act to amend the Criminal Code* was tabled in the House of Commons on December 12, 1991, and passed into law as S.C. 1992. c. 38 in June 1993. This Act restructured legal meanings of consent and limitations on the introduction of evidence concerning past sexual history.

. . . .

Delia Opekokew, a Cree woman from Saskatchewan, was the first Native woman admitted to the bar in Ontario in 1983. In 1979, she became the first Native woman admitted to the bar in Saskatchewan. She has worked, *inter alia*, on land claims litigation (*The [Toronto] Globe and Mail* [26 February 1994], p. A10C).

1984

Anne Clare Cools became the first black woman appointed to the Senate of Canada.

. . . .

Marva Jemmott was appointed as a Queen's Counsel, the first black woman to receive this distinction. She graduated from the University of Ottawa in Common Law in 1969.

. . . .

Pauktuutit, The Inuit Women's Association of Canada, was founded. Its focus is on family violence, violence against women, and child sexual abuse (Canadian Advisory on the Status of Women, *Expanding Our Horizons: The Work of the Canadian Advisory Council on the Status of Women*, Ottawa, 1993, p. 133).

. . . .

The first (and only) televised debate on women's issues between the three major parties during a federal election campaign was held. It was organized by NAC and picketed by R.E.A.L. Women (Canadian Advisory on the Status of Women, *Expanding Our Horizons: The Work of the Canadian Advisory Council on the Status of Women*, Ottawa, 1993, p. 132).

. . . .

The Ontario *Royal Commission on Equality in Employment*, headed by Rosalie Abella, tabled its report in the House of Commons. It recommended "employment equity."

. . . .

Mothers are Women (MAW) was founded in 1984. MAW is a group of women who "have chosen (and admit they can afford to choose) to stay at home with their children, despite education and training (mainly for professional occupations)." Most of its members "consider themselves feminists" but the organization has been ideologically at odds with NAC. In the early 1980s, NAC's approach was based on the premise that "the integration of women into the public sphere of paid work is the appropriate, ultimate goal." Members of MAW did not consider this approach to "reflect their views or their interests." In 1987, however, MAW successfully challenged NAC's views on the "stay-at-home" mother and NAC developed an understanding of women's work at home. MAW was admitted to NAC and then succeeded in having a "task force established to consider the issues involved." While NAC saw tax benefits given directly to parents in the paid labour force as the "least effective way of developing a system of quality child care services in Canada," MAW argued that a policy that extended "public support for child care to women in the paid workforce but not one that extended similar support to women who worked at home" was discriminatory to the "stay-at-home" mother (Vickers, pp. 252, 258, 262–63).

MAW is currently leading the campaign to get unpaid work counted in the 1996 Census. The exclusion of unpaid work from official data sources stems from the United Nations System of National Accounts which was developed in the 1950s. Economic production excludes household work because it is assumed that households consume rather than produce. Statistics Canada estimated that the value of unpaid domestic work in 1992 was between $210.7 and 318.8 billion dollars, or 30–45 per cent of the Gross Domestic Product. "The lower estimate is based on the replacement cost, which is what it would have cost to purchase these services. The higher estimate is based on opportunity cost, the amount that Canadians could have earned on the labour market had they not been tied up with unpaid chores." Women do more unpaid work than men. MAW argues that because there are no questions in the Census concerning unpaid work that those who do unpaid work "disappear." Consequently, government policy is developed that directly affects women who work in the home yet does not consider their needs. For example, divorce settlements and Victims Compensation Board settlements are affected if they do not give value to unpaid work at home; transportation policy that is geared towards members of the paid labour force only; child care policy; and social service funding cutbacks that result in additional burdens on women in the home (Vanier Institute of the Family, *Transition*, vol. 24, no. 2, June 1994, pp. 5–6).

1985

On April 17, the equality section of the Charter of Rights, section 15, comes into force. On the same day, a national organization committed to actualising women's equality through legal education and action was formed:

> On April 17, 1985, the Women's Legal Education and Action Fund (LEAF) was formed by women in recognition that *it* was one thing to have equality on paper and quite another to have it as a reality. LEAF was established with...the objective of promoting women's equality in the courts. LEAF has come to play a central role as an innovative feminist organization initiating and coordinating women's legal advocacy in Canada. The cases it is or has been involved in range across a spectrum of issues affecting older women, aboriginal and immigrant women, lesbians, and women's concerns with welfare benefits, reproduction and policing.
>
> Funding to LEAF is provided through donated legal services, the Ontario litigation fund established in 1985 for LEAF's Ontario litigation, and through fundraising activities. Core funding for the national office and staffing has been provided by the Secretary of State.

LEAF has developed an approach to equality which emphasises the reality of women's lives and the importance of looking at the impact of legislation, policy and government action on women. The way women are oppressed in Canadian society forms the basis of sex discrimination. And LEAF has been careful not to advance equality for women at the expense of other oppressed groups — the goal is equality for all disadvantaged groups. Indeed, most women are disadvantaged in more than one way. LEAF's theory and cases work to make equality a reality for all women in Canada and not just women who are white and middle class. The approach is meaningful and involved because it is the lives of the women affected by the issue that the cases are all about.

Thus far LEAF has been very successful. It has more than 300 active files and has received positive outcomes through litigation and settlement on a consistent basis. It has become part of the mosaic of the Canadian women's community (Brettel Dawson, "LEAF" [1989] 10:5 *Broadside* at 6). [as modified by the author]

. . . .

The first issue of the *Canadian Journal of Women and the Law* was published. The journal has an editorial board with a national, bilingual and interdisciplinary emphasis. The following extract is taken from the inaugural "Editorial" of the Canadian Journal of Women and the Law.

Editorial*

Even though this is but the first issue of the Canadian Journal of Women and the Law, the journal already has a long history. The idea was first raised in 1982 by Ruth Lipton, then a law student and member of NAWL at the University of Windsor. Later that year, Monique Charlebois, then a member of the NAWL steering committee, and Kathleen Lahey, a law teacher at the University of Windsor, began to formulate the first working proposals for the new publication. Two different proposals were developed and submitted to funding sources: a proposal for a multidisciplinary journal like this, and a proposal for a women's law reporter that would collect cases and statutory material from across the country and organize them in a major reporting service. A great deal of work was actually done on the reporting service, and that project still seems to us to be of crucial importance. Funding sources consistently decided that they would prefer to support a journal, however, so NAWL has deferred the development of the reporter. We settled upon a journal format that would give legal workers, activists, researchers, and academics a fair amount of choice as to the length and type of papers to submit and that would enable us to publish material which reflects the wide range of approaches that are being taken to the complex topic of "women and the law."

. . . .

We are particularly pleased that the actual publication of the journal has begun in 1985 — the year in which all of the quality provisions of the Charter of Rights and Freedoms have finally become effective. We consider this to be an important event in the development of feminist publishing for several other reasons as well. We think that the contents of this issue reflect the multidisciplinary nature

of women's studies — at least half of the major articles have been contributed by women who work in history, sociology, education, philosophy, and human rights. We are strongly committed to maintaining and developing this multidisciplinary format; just as individuals working in isolation cannot solve the problems that women face in today's world, so adequate solutions cannot be developed within the narrow scope of any one discipline.

. . . .

As we embark on the process of claiming equality as a concept that has meaning for women as well as for men, and as we begin the publication of a journal that has as one of its ultimate aims the transformation of the normative tradition itself, we are aware that this project is situated within deep contradictions in the liberal tradition. Women are oppressed by the content of the law as well as by the ideas and conduct of many lawyers, judges, legislators, and law teachers, yet we have chosen to work within the legal process — as other women have chosen to work within other cultural institutions — in the struggle for liberation. We are aware that putting this much energy into an "academic" project may ultimately divert our energies from other urgent tasks; all struggles carry with them that risk. However, we are confirmed in our decision to publish this journal by the many women who have generously assisted us in the preparation of this issue and by the many women who are actively engaged in feminist legal scholarship. We also feel confident that our readers will give us the kind of guidance that will ensure that this journal serves the needs of the women's movement as completely as possible, for this is not our journal — it is yours.

. . . .

Section 12(1)(b) of the *Indian Act* which stripped status from status-Indian women who married non-status Indian men was repealed and replaced with a complex set of new criteria. The Native Women's Association of Canada, stated in their Organization Statement, (updated, April 1990): "It has been over four years since the Indian Act was amended and it continues

to be a major area of concern to us. The amended Indian Act continues to be an oppressive piece of Canadian legislation that only further entrenches discrimination, and in fact, threatens our future generations." The amendment is also being challenged by Indian men as a violation of band control of membership as provided in the Indian Act (*Twigg*).

. . . .

Manitoba became the first province in Canada to pass "pay equity" legislation designed to ensure that workers received equal pay for work of equal value: *The Pay Equity Act*, C.C.S.M., c. P.13. The federal *Employment Equity Act* S.C. 1986 was proclaimed into law in 1986 and provides voluntary guidelines involving pay equity

and other matters of equity in employment. The federal contractors programme put in place at the same time was designed to require compliance by organizations receiving federal contracts. Ontario passed the *Pay Equity Act* in 1987 (now R.S.O. 1990, c. P.7), and established a Pay Equity Commission in 1987. The

---

* "Editorial" (1985) 1 Can. J. Women and the Law 1 at iv. Extracts. Reprinted by permission of the Canadian Journal of Women and the Law.

Ontario legislation "is the first proactive pay equity programme in North America to extend to the private sector."

[See further, Debra J. Lewis, *Just Give Us the Money* (Vancouver: Women's Research Centre, 1988).]

. . . .

The DisAbled Women's Network was founded in 1985. DAWN Canada was the first feminist disability organization "to tackle and bring forth the issues impacting women with disabilities who were victims/survivors of violence." At the founding meeting in June 1985, it was decided that priority must be given to the following issues: "violence against women with disabilities, access to the women's movement and services, the provision of role models for young girls with disabilities, as well as issues related to self-image and parenting." Since that meeting, 19 local and provincial DAWN groups have been organized. Its focus on access to the women's movement has resulted in women's conferences becoming more accessible to disabled

women. DAWN has also produced many reports on issues affecting women with disabilities and its members have become recognized by government, women's organizations and disabled-rights groups as experts on disabled women's issues. The national office of DAWN Canada closed, however, in March 1993 due to "substantial cuts in the project funding received from the Secretary of State...funding cuts at the national level will not directly affect local chapters of DAWN, which are provincially funded, but these local chapters have now lost the centre of their network" (Pat Israel and Fran Odette, "The Disabled Women's Movement, 1983 to 1993," *Canadian Woman Studies* 13, no. 4 [1993], 6–8).

1986

The National Organization of Immigrant and Visible Minority Women of Canada was founded. Its goal is to advance equality for immigrant and visible minority women (Canadian Advisory on the Status of Women,

Expanding Our Horizons: The Work of the Canadian Advisory Council on the Status of Women, Ottawa, 1993, p. 134).

. . . .

Shirley Carr became the first woman elected president of the Canadian Labour Congress. In 1974, she was

elected the first woman executive vice-president of the CLC (Armour, pp. 99, 134).

1987

Canada's first black woman judge was appointed, when Corrine Sparks was appointed to the family court in Nova Scotia. In 1979, she had been the first black

woman to graduate in law school from Dalhousie University in Halifax (*Excellence Magazine*, July/August 1987).

1988

Immigrant and Visible Minority Women Against Abuse was founded. Objectives are to "raise awareness among immigrant women about the problem of abuse, build solidarity with abused women, and network with

other organizations that share the same goal of ending violence against women" (Canadian Council on Social Development, *Vis-à-vis* [A National Newsletter on Family Violence], 12, no. 1 [Summer 1994], 9).

. . . .

On January 28, 1988, the Supreme Court of Canada struck down as unconstitutional, the restrictions on abortion contained in section 251 of the *Criminal Code*. The section was held to deprive women of their constitutionally guaranteed right to "life, liberty, and security of the person." Chief Justice Dickson concluded that "forcing a woman, by threat of criminal sanction, to carry a foetus to term unless she meets certain criteria unrelated to her own priorities and

aspirations, is a profound interference with a woman's body and thus a violation of security of the person" (*Morgentaler* v. *The Queen* (1988), 82 N.R. 1 at 24). Madame Justice Wilson went further, concluding that the section violated women's liberty. She commented:

> The State will respect choices made by individuals, and, to the greatest extent possible, will avoid subordinating these choices to any

one conception of the good life...an aspect of the respect for human dignity...is the right to make fundamental personal decisions without interference from the State. (7)

The right to liberty...guarantees to every individual a degree of personal autonomy over important decisions intimately affecting their private lives...the decision of a woman to terminate her pregnancy falls within this class of protected decisions...it will have profound psychological, economic and social consequences for the pregnant woman...it is a decision that deeply reflects the way a woman feels about herself and her relationship to others and to society at large. It is not just a medical decision; it is a profound social and ethical one as well. Her response to it will be the response of the whole person.... It is probably impossible for a man to respond, even imaginatively, to such a dilemma not just because it is outside the realm of his experience (although this is, of course, the case) but because he can relate to it only by objectifying it, thereby eliminating the subjective elements of the female psyche which are at the heart of the dilemma...women's rights are only now being translated into protected rights. The right to reproduce...is one such right and is properly perceived as an integral part of modern woman's struggle to assert her dignity and worth as a human being.

. . . .

August 25: The National Council of the Canadian Bar Association adopted a resolution calling on the federal government to establish a Task Force on Gender Equality. The companion "Rationale for a National Task Force on Gender Equality in the Courts and in the Law," noted that such a recommendation was consistent with the Abella *Commission on Employment Equity* (1984), the Parliamentary Committee on Equality Rights, "Toward Equality — The Response of the Report of the Parliamentary Committee on Equality Rights" (1986), and the proceedings of the 1986 Banff Conference, "Equality and Judicial Neutrality." All of these sources had identified instances of systemic discrimination on the basis of sex either in substantive law or in the administration of the Canadian legal system. Moreover, some twenty-five states in the United States have established such Task Forces. Three of these task forces have submitted reports to date and they "have concluded that differential treatment on the basis of gender was widespread — affecting not only differential treatment of female judges, attorneys, court personnel, litigants and witnesses, but also the outcome of certain types of litigation" (Companion Rationale, at 2).

Gender Equality in the Courts*

WHEREAS the Canadian Bar Association is committed to the principle of equality for women and men in the legal system of Canada; and

WHEREAS many states in the United States have either completed or begun investigation of their legal systems in order to identify and remedy any discriminatory treatment of men and women in their legal systems; and

WHEREAS there have been fragmented attempts to address the issue of gender equality in the Canadian legal system; and

WHEREAS the Charter of Rights and Freedoms guarantees all Canadians freedom from discrimination based on gender;

BE IT RESOLVED that the Canadian Bar Association urge the Federal government to establish a Task Force on Gender Equality to:

(1) investigate whether or what gender discrimination, exist in the Canadian legal system; and

(2) make recommendations to eliminate gender discrimination in the Canadian legal system.

. . . .

November: The Manitoba Association of Women and the Law issued a report entitled *Gender Equality in the Courts*, which examined U.S. Task Forces on Gender Equality and studied areas of family law (custody and support orders, matrimonial property division) and tort law (personal injury damages) in light of concerns of bias. Gender unfairness was defined as

an unacknowledged phenomenon in judicial decision making and in the treatment of

---

* Text of Resolution No. 3, passed by the National Council of the Canadian Bar Association, Montreal, 25 August 1988.

women litigants, women attorneys and women court personnel which negatively affects women's lives. In the United States, gender bias has been described as "attitudes and behaviours based on sex stereotypes, the perceived relative worth of women and men, and myths and misconceptions about the economic and social problems encountered by both sexes. It is reflected in attitudes and behaviours toward women and men which are based on stereotyped beliefs about the nature and roles of the sexes rather than upon independent valuation of individual ability, life experiences and aspirations." (Lynne Hecht Schafran, "Establishing A Gender Bias Task Force" (1987) 4 Law and Inequality 103).

The Report concluded that

a two-fold approach is necessary to eliminate gender unfairness in the Canadian judicial system. It is possible to proceed concurrently with both approaches.

(1) A substantive education programme on gender unfairness should immediately be commenced
(2) A National Task Force on Gender Equality in the Courts should be established. (33)

The Canadian Bar Association established a Gender Bias Task Force in 1992, chaired by now retired Supreme Court judge, Hon. Bertha Wilson. The Task Force reported in 1993.

. . . .

Ethel Blondin was elected to the House of Commons as the Liberal member for the Western Arctic. She was the first Aboriginal woman to be elected to the federal Parliament and sat as the only Aboriginal woman M.P. She was the Liberal Party critic for Aboriginal Affairs. Prior to her election, Blondin was an assistant deputy minister in the Department of Community Relations in the Government of the Northwest Territories. In 1993, she was appointed Minister of State for Youth and Training and became the first Aboriginal woman to be appointed to the federal cabinet.

1989

The Supreme Court of Canada handed down its first decisions on equality in relation to women under section 15 of the Charter of Rights.

In *Andrews* v. *Law Society for British Columbia*, [1989] 1 S.C.R. 143, a challenge was made to legislation which allowed only Canadian citizens to practice law. In *Andrews*, the judge emphasised that a "bad law will not be saved merely because it operates equally upon those to whom it has application." Instead, he advocated an approach which considers "the content of the law, to its purpose, and its impact upon those to whom it applies, and also upon those whom it excludes from its application." The systemic nature of discrimination against women and the gender specific nature of experience formed the basis of the decisions of *Janzen* v. *Platy Enterprises*, [1989] 1 S.C.R. 1252, dealing with sexual harassment and *Brooks* v. *Canada Safeway Ltd*, [1989] 1 S.C.R. 1219, dealing with employment benefits for pregnancy women.

In *Janzen*, the Chief Justice, Brian Dickson, commented:

clearly a person who is disadvantaged because of her sex, is being discriminated against in her employment when [the] employer conduct denies her financial rewards because of her sex, or exacts some form of sexual compliance to improve or maintain her existing benefits. The evil to be remedied is the utilization of economic power or authority so as to restrict a woman's guaranteed and equal access to the workplace, and all of its benefits, free from extraneous pressures having to do with the mere fact that she is a woman. Where a woman's equal access is denied or when terms or conditions differ when compared to male employees, the woman is being discriminated against.

And, in *Brooks*, he said:

It is difficult to conceive that distinctions or discriminations based upon pregnancy could ever be regarded as other than discrimination based upon sex, or that restrictive statutory conditions applicable only to pregnant women did not discriminate against them as women.... The capacity to become pregnant is unique to the female gender. A distinction based on pregnancy is not merely a distinction between those who are and are not pregnant, but also between the gender that has the capacity for pregnancy and the gender which does not.

In these decisions, the Supreme Court of Canada has indicated a break with the interpretative approach taken to section 1 of the *Bill of Rights*, and rejected, to some extent, the "similarly situate" test used in U.S. sex discrimination law. The effect of Brooks was also to over-rule the 1978 decision in *Bliss* v. *A.G. for Canada* (*supra*).

An interesting sidelight on legal attitudes to pregnancy occurred in Australia toward the end of 1988 "when a planning decision of the Victorian Administrative Appeals Tribunal was challenged in the Supreme Court on the novel ground that a member of the tribunal was five months pregnant when making the decision."

Pregnant Tribunals*

The proposition seemed absurd that a tribunal would purport to exercise wide discretions while pregnant.   (Affidavit of Garry Bigmore)

Towards the end of 1988 a planning decision of the Victorian Administrative Appeals Tribunal was challenged in the Supreme Court on the novel ground that a member of the tribunal was five months pregnant when making the decision (*GTB Nominees Pty. Ltd.* v. *Uniting Church Property Trust in Australia and City of Kew*, Supreme Court of Victoria, 25 January 1989). The grounds of appeal (under the *Administrative Appeals Tribunal Act*) included the allegation that, when the presiding member heard the case and gave her decision, she "suffered from the well-known medical condition ('placidity') which detracts significantly from the intellectual competence of all mothers-to-be." The applicant claimed that he had therefore been denied natural justice, on the ground of bias.

The applicant was Garry Bigmore, a Melbourne solicitor who had been one of the objectors at the AAT hearing into plans to rebuild part of a nursing home in a quiet affluent street in prestigious Kew. Mr. Bigmore had been acting for himself. He obtained legal advice as the matter was about to proceed and the appeal was then abandoned. Nonetheless he later repeated his criticisms of the tribunal to the waiting journalists outside the court, and to George Negus on the "Today" television program.

Mr. Bigmore, apparently unembarrassed by the implications of his action, said in an affidavit, "Had I become aware of Ms. Smith's pregnancy during the course of the hearing, I would have immediately suspected a likelihood of bias or incompetence on the part of the tribunal." He is also quoted in the *Age* (26.1.89) as stating, "the proposition seemed absurd that a tribunal would purport to exercise wide discretions while pregnant."

The president of the Equal Opportunity Board, Margaret Rizkalla, who had worked as a lawyer and as a magistrate through her two pregnancies, was astounded by the claim that pregnancy could affect a woman's competence to make a decision. She had not heard of such a claim being used

to discriminate against someone; "You would just boggle at it, wouldn't you?" (*Age* 26.1.89).

Suspending disbelief for a moment, however, what would the legal position have been if the case had run? It is clear that, to establish bias in a tribunal such as the AAT, there must be at least a "reasonable apprehension" of bias (*Livesey v. NSW Bar Association* (1983), 151 CLR 288). This commonly means a pecuniary interest, for instance, or a known prejudice which could reasonably be seen as creating an interest in the success of one party. It is not easily shown. There is no expectation that decision makers have no views of their own, or that they will be "devoid of any sense of moral or social direction"; the issue is "whether persuasion is a genuine possibility" (Aronson and Franklin, *Review of Administrative Action*, 1987, p. 196).

And what was the bias complained of? Mr. Bigmore in his affidavit stated his belief that because of her pregnancy, Ms. Smith "might well be unduly biased in favour of a non-profit organization looking after very old people." One letter writer commented on this assertion, "why would Ms. Smith be likely to favour a nursing home? A maternity wing, may be..." (*Age* 4.2.89). Why indeed might she not favour the interests of nearby home owners? And what of Ms. Smith's (male) colleague on the AAT, who also found in favour of the nursing home?

There was no suggestion that Mr. Bigmore or his fellow objectors made any objection on the ground of bias during the AAT hearing (although Ms. Smith was visibly pregnant). Nor was there any objection made at the hearing about the manner in which it was conducted by Ms. Smith and her colleague, over a period of three days. Further, it was not suggested that there was any evidence that Ms. Smith personally suffered from a peculiar condition known to have affected her mental competence at that time.

The argument was, simply, that all pregnant women are intellectually incompetent! This is unsupportable. But even if it could be argued, it would not provide an argument as to bias.

* Bronwyn Naylor, "Pregnant Tribunals" (1989) 14 Legal Service Bulletin at 41–42. Reprinted by permission of Legal Service Bulletin, Monash University, Australia.

Mr. Bigmore cited in support of his assertion of incompetence a passage from Derek Llewellyn-Jones' book *Everywoman*, which says that the pregnant woman "notes an increasing placidity and drowsiness as pregnancy advances." She "no longer has the clarity of mind and precision of thought she had before pregnancy.... She will have to look inwards into the warmth of her womb, rather than attempting to equal Einstein!" This was the basis of his claim that the AAT member's intellectual competence had been reduced.

Few other gynaecologists agree that such a condition exists. And recent doctoral research by Zevia Schneider, a midwife educator, gives a different picture. The women studied, most of whom worked through their pregnancy, if anything showed *improved* performance in a series of regular cognitive tests during pregnancy. Although they all complained that they suffered lapses of concentration or mem-

ory, the tests showed the opposite (*Age* 27.1.89). Ms. Schneider observed, however, that many Melbourne midwives accepted the myth that women are less competent during pregnancy, and that women themselves sometimes contributed to the myth, by suggesting they were not functioning as well during pregnancy, and occasionally lagging in mood and motivation.

Pregnant women, particularly in the late stages, sometimes say they are distracted by the thought of the imminent changes, lifestyle changes and so on. Just as people going through relationship breakup, dealing with death in the family, moving house or renovating are likely to feel distracted. This is not to say they become less competent, or lose their skills. It is not a question of competence, or bias. GTB Nominees was an attempted remake of an old movie, *Biology as Destiny*. In this case even the backers withdrew before it had the chance to flop.

. . . .

What could be called a "summer of discontent" erupted in courts across Canada, as attempts were made by men to obtain injunctions preventing women from legally terminating their pregnancies.

In the first case, *Murphy* v. *Dodd* (July 4, 1989) (Ont. H.C., O'Driscoll J.), the first instance judge granted an injunction to the former boyfriend of a pregnant woman to prevent her from obtaining an abortion. The injunction was quickly set aside on technical grounds on 12 July 1989 (Supreme Court of Ontario, Gray J.).

The second case, *Tremblay* v. *Daigle*, [1989] 2 S.C.R. 530, held the nation, by and large, riveted in high drama as a first instance judge granted a similar injunction to a former boyfriend (a jilted ex-lover in media parlance) to prevent a woman from terminating her pregnancy. On appeal, the Quebec Court of Appeal upheld the injunction. The matter was taken on an emergency basis to the Supreme Court of Canada, which first gave leave to appeal and a week later heard the arguments on appeal from the parties' lawyers and various intervenors representing pro-choice and anti-abortion interests. In Montreal, 10,000 people rallied in support of Chantal Daigle, the woman subject to the injunction. During the course of the hearing, a bombshell was dropped when Daigle's lawyer informed the judges that Daigle had terminated

her pregnancy. (Later, it was learned that Daigle had travelled to Boston several days before the hearing. She was in her 21st week of pregnancy by that time.) The judges decided that the matter was not moot and continued to hear argument. At the end of the day, they gave their decision to vacate the injunction but reserved their reasons. When their unanimous reasons were ultimately released, Chief Justice Dickson, for the court, held that according to civil and common law, the fetus has no legal status and purported "fathers" have no rights on behalf either of the fetus or of themselves to seek intervention to prevent the woman from having an abortion.

Subsequently, two other attempts were reportedly made by anti-abortionists to prevent pregnant women from obtaining legal terminations. In one, a Manitoba judge threw out an application by a former boyfriend when it was apparent that the woman was not in fact pregnant. ("Judge denies man bid to halt abortion," *The [Toronto] Globe and Mail* [14 February 1990] A3.) In the second, the indefatigable lawyer who had represented Gregory Murphy and argued for R.E.A.L. Women of Canada in the Supreme Court in *Tremblay* v. *Daigle*, sought to test the limits of the Supreme Court of Canada decision by bringing another case in Ontario. She reportedly received short shrift from the judge.

. . . .

October 25, 1989: A Royal Commission on New Reproductive Technologies was established by the federal government. Lobbying by the feminist-oriented Canadian Coalition for a Royal Commission on New

Reproductive Technologies, established in 1987, played a significant role in encouraging the government to establish the Royal Commission. The Commission reported in 1993.

A Royal Commission on New Reproductive Technologies*

THE MANDATE

The Commission will be established under Part I of the Inquiries Act and will inquire into and report on current and potential medical and scientific developments related to new reproductive technologies, considering in particular their social, ethical, health, research, legal and economic implications and the public interest, recommending what policies and safeguards should be applied.

The Commission will examine in particular:

(a)   implications of new reproductive technologies for women's reproductive health and well-being;

(b)   the causes, treatment and prevention of male and female infertility;

(c)   reversals of sterilization procedures, artificial insemination, *in vitro* fertilization, embryo, transfers, prenatal screening and diagnostic techniques, genetic manipulation and therapeutic interventions to correct genetic anomalies, sex selection techniques, embryo experimentation and fetal tissue transplants;

(d)   social and legal arrangements, such as surrogate child-bearing, judicial interventions during gestation and birth, and "ownership" of ova, sperm, embryos and fetal tissue;

(e)   the status and rights of people using or contributing to reproductive services, such as access to procedures, "rights" to parenthood, informed consent, status of gamete donors and confidentiality, and the impact of these services on all concerned parties, particularly the children; and

(f)   the economic ramifications of these technologies, such as the commercial marketing of ova, sperm and embryos, the application of patent law, and the funding of research and procedures including infertility treatment.

• • • •

November 3, 1989: Bill C-43, *An Act Respecting Abortion* was introduced by the federal government into the House of Commons. On May 29, 1990, the House of Commons passed the Bill on a free vote (although cabinet ministers were required to vote for the government's legislation) by a nine-vote margin. The legislation provides:

1. Sections 287 and 288 of the *Criminal Code* are repealed and the following substituted therefor:

"**287.**(1) Every *person who induces an abortion on a female person* is guilty of an indictable offence and liable to imprisonment for *a term not exceeding two years*, unless the abortion is induced by or under the direction of a medical practitioner who is of the opinion that, if the abortion were not induced, the health or life of the female person would be likely to be threatened.

(2) For the purposes of this section, "health" includes, for greater certainty, physical, mental and psychological health;

"medical practitioner," in respect of an abortion induced in a province, means a person who is entitled to practise medicine under the laws of that province;

"opinion" means an opinion formed using generally accepted standards of the medical profession.

(3) For the purposes of this section and section 288, inducing an abortion does not include using a drug, device or other means on a female person that is likely to prevent implantation of a fertilized ovum.

288. Every one who unlawfully supplies or procures a drug or other noxious thing or an instrument or thing, knowing that it is intended to be used or employed to *induce an abortion on* a female person, is guilty of an indictable offence and liable to imprisonment for a term not exceeding two years."

The Bill was defeated when it received a tie vote in the Senate later that year. No other legislation on the matter has since been introduced.

• • • •

Roberta Jamieson was the first Native woman appointed Ombudsman of Ontario.

---

* Office of the Prime Minister, Press Release (25 October 1989) "Prime Minister Announces Royal Commission on Reproductive Technologies."

Glenda Simms became the first black woman appointed president of CACSW.

. . . .

December 6, 1989: A young armed man walked into the engineering building of L'Ecole Polytechnique de Montreal, in Montreal, in the early evening of the last day of classes for the semester. He stalked the halls and cafeteria, shooting women. Then he entered a classroom, and ordered the men in the room to leave. He ordered the women to gather in one section of the room, yelling, "you're all a bunch of feminists" and then proceeded to shoot the women. By the time his ammunition was expended and he had turned his gun on himself, he had murdered 14 women and injured 14 more. This massacre was profoundly political and profoundly shocking. December 6 has been declared a National Day of Memorial. Since the killings, gun control legislation has been more actively pursued and national debates on violence against women, women's safety and women in higher education have been framed in sharp relief.

The text of the killer's letter as reproduced follows:

Text of Lépine's Letter*

This is the text of Marc Lépine's letter which was sent to La Presse columnist Francine Pelletier.

Forgive the mistakes, I only had 15 minutes to write it.

See also Annex.

Please note that if I am committing suicide today 89/12/06 it is not for economic reasons (for I have waited until I exhausted all my financial means, even refusing jobs) but for political reasons. For I have decided to send Ad Patres the feminists who have always ruined my life. It has been seven years that life does not bring me any joy and being totally blasè, I have decided to put an end to those viragos.

I had already tried in my youth to enlist in the Forces as an officer cadet, which would have allowed me to enter the arsenal and precede Lortie in a rampage. They refused me because asocial. So I waited until this day to execute all my projects. In between, I continued my studies in a haphazard way for they never really interested me, knowing in advance my fate. Which did not prevent me from obtaining very good marks despite not handing in my theory works and the lack of studying before exams.

Even if the Mad Killer epithet will be attributed to me by the media, I consider myself a rational erudite (person) that only the arrival of the Grim Reaper has forced to take extreme acts. For why persevere to exist if it is only to please the government. Being rather backward-looking by nature (except for science), the feminists always have a talent to enrage me. They want to keep the advantages of women (e.g. cheaper insurance, extended maternity leave preceded by a preventive retreat) while trying to grab those of the men.

Thus it is an obvious truth that if the Olympic Games removed the Men/Women distinction, there would be Women only in the graceful events. So the feminists are not fighting to remove that barrier. They are so opportunistic they neglect to profit from the knowledge accumulated by men through the ages. They always try to misrepresent them every time they can. Thus, the other day, I heard they were honoring the Canadian men and women who fought at the frontline during the world wars. How can you explain then that women then were not authorized to go to the frontline??? Will we hear of Caesar's female legions and female galley slaves who of course took up 50 per cent of the ranks of history, though they never existed. A real Casus Belli.

Sorry for this too brief letter.

Marc Lépine

The letter is followed by the 19-name list, with a note at the bottom:

Nearly died today. The lack of time (because I started too late.) has allowed those radical feminists to survive.

Alea Jacta Est

---

* Translation published in *The [Montreal] Gazette* (24 November 1990), A2.

The mentioned annex was left out as a condition, requested by F. Pelletier, for the release of the letter. The names of the women Marc Lépine murdered are as follows:

Geneviève Bergeron	Maryse Laganière	Annie St.-Arneault	Barbara Maria Kueznick
Maude Haviernick	Barbara Daigneault	Maryse Leclaire	Ann-Marie Lemay
Michèle Richard	Ann-Marie Edward	Hélène Colgan	Sonia Pelletier
Nathalie Crotaeau	Annie Turcotte		

1990

Hon. Audrey McLaughlin was selected as leader of the federal New Democratic Party — the first woman to lead a major political party in North America. In the 1993 federal election her party won only nine seats. She announced her resignation in 1994. Alexa McDonough had been the first woman to lead a provincial party when she was elected leader of the Nova Scotia New Democratic Party in 1980. The first woman leader of a political party was Thérèse Casgrain who, in 1951, led the Co-operative Commonwealth Federation in Quebec.

. . . .

February 8: Madame Justice Wilson of the Supreme Court of Canada delivered the Barbara Betcherman Memorial Lecture at Osgoode Hall Law School in Toronto. In her speech, entitled "Will Women Judges Really Make a Difference?", Wilson J. argued that areas of law had been distorted by gender bias and that a national Task Force on Gender Equality should be established.

This speech prompted a complaint to the Canadian Judicial Council against the judge by R.E.A.L. Women of Canada. The complaint was dismissed without investigation. The following letter, written by a Toronto lawyer, appeared in the *Toronto Star*.

Justice Wilson Held Audience Spellbound*

Re REAL Women and Madam Justice Bertha Wilson: You had to be there.

Madam Justice Bertha Wilson of the Supreme Court of Canada rose in the Moot Courtroom at Osgoode Hall Law School recently to speak on the difference which the appointment of women to judicial positions might make in our legal system. The hall was packed. An overflow crowd filled an adjoining classroom.

Justice Wilson spoke from a lengthy and carefully prepared text. The speech bristled with quotations. Theories of judicial impartiality from authors as diverse as Socrates and Judge Rosalie Abella were quoted and explored. The lecture was a scholarly and judicial tour de force.

Justice Wilson spoke for well over an hour in that dry, precise, largely uninflected, tone that is so personal to her. At the end of the speech the room erupted in a standing, cheering ovation. I have never seen an argument of such breadth and subtlety communicated with such direct and simple force.

Nor was the argument anything as simplistic as wholesale condemnation of gender bias in the legal system. Justice Wilson believes firmly that courts and legal systems must be free from all bias. Only when a gender bias has unthinkingly crept into the system does an issue arise.

There are feminist thinkers who would take the analysis much further. They would argue, with some thought-provoking examples, that areas of our law which we presume to be entirely gender neutral (contract law, for example) have in fact been constructed out of the life experiences of men and would be quite different had they been developed by women for women's purposes.

Justice Wilson believes in a better world than that, a world in which men and women on the bench, in business and in their private lives can discern their own gender biases and remove them from their legal, commercial and personal actions.

To find this scholarly and challenging analysis turned into a complaint by REAL Women to the Judicial Council that Justice Wilson is herself biased is profoundly disappointing. It is also pathetically stupid. Justice Wilson is as astute as any member of the bench in Canada. Not only would she void bias in her judgments and actions, she

---

* Brian Bucknall, Letter to the Editor, *Toronto Star* (17 February 1990).

76

would avoid any choice of words which could be interpreted as showing bias. One glance by the Judicial Council at the text of her speech will demonstrate that REAL Women have not comprehended, or even tried to comprehend, the thrust of the argument. To consciously distort a serious intellectual discourse for the purposes of a cheap publicity stunt is a despicable act.

. . . .

March: The Hon. Kim Campbell was appointed to the federal cabinet, becoming the first woman to serve as federal Minister of Justice and Attorney-General. She was quoted at the time as saying:

I make no apologies for the fact that I am a feminist and that I think it is important that I bring with me, into the Ministry, my outlook on the world. I hope that people will be able to identify a difference that was made by a woman Minister of Justice. (Quoted in Brad Daisley, "New Minister proud of 'feminist' view of justice," *The Lawyer's Weekly* [27 April 1990] 6.)

. . . .

In 1990, Zanana Akande, a New Democratic Party candidate, became the first black woman elected to the provincial legislature of Ontario, when she was elected in the Toronto riding of St Andrew-St Patrick. Akande, an educator and long time activist with social agencies such as the United Way, the Meals on Wheels program and several feminist organizations, was quoted at the time of her election as saying:

That target is to effect a political situation and a society where business and the common citizen can exist and prosper.... I do not feel pressure to say "Tomorrow it's going to be our way".... I think you have to work within the existing social infrastructure to change it and you do not throw everything out.... When the interests of my race must be spoken to, I'll speak for them.... When the issues of my sex have to be spoken to, I'll speak to them too. But not to the exclusion of everything else. ("School principal Akande graduates to Queen's Park," *Toronto Star* [12 September 1990] A13.)

Akande was also the first black woman to become a member of the Ontario cabinet. Her experience in politics and Cabinet was bruising and Akande announced in advance of the next election that she would not stand again.

1991

February 20: Terry Vyse became the first Aboriginal woman to be appointed as judge in Ontario when she was appointed to the Provincial Court of Ontario. Vyse had been a lawyer in private practice in St. Catherines, Ontario. She was the first Aboriginal person appointed to the bench in Ontario.

. . . .

Nellie Cournoyea, became the first Aboriginal woman elected as government leader of a territory (NWT). In 1992 Rosemary Kuptana, of the Inuit Tapirisat, and Nellie Cournoyea, NWT government leader, were the first Aboriginal women to participate in official constitutional negotiations.

1992

Paule Gauthier became the first woman president of the Canadian Bar Association (Canadian Advisory on the Status of Women, *Expanding Our Horizons: The Work of the Canadian Advisory Council on the Status of Women*, Ottawa, 1993, p. 137).

1993

Ardyth Cooper became the first Aboriginal woman to hold a senior executive position in the Canadian Advisory Council on the Status of Women (Western vice-president) (Canadian Advisory Council on the Status of Women, *Annual Report 1992–1993*, p. 12).

. . . .

Sunera Thobani was the first woman of colour to be elected as president of NAC. Thobani was accused of being an illegal immigrant by John McDougall, Tory M.P. Her White predecessor, Judy Rebick, was also an immigrant to Canada (from the United States) but was never accused of the same.

. . . .

Jean Augustine became the first black woman to be elected to the House of Commons, when she was elected Liberal M.P. for a Toronto riding.

. . . .

Catherine Callbeck became the first woman elected as provincial premier, when she led the Liberal Party to victory in Prince Edward Island. She was first elected to the PEI Legislative Assembly in 1974 and was appointed Minister of Health and Social Services, Minister Responsible for the Disabled, 1974–78. She left politics to work in the family business, Callbeck's Ltd, in 1978 and did not return until 1988 when she served as opposition critic for Consumer and Corporate Affairs, Energy Mines and Resources, and Financial Institutions (*Who's Who in Canada*, pp. 101–102).

The first woman to become a provincial premier was Rita Johnson, who assumed the party leadership of the Social Credit Party in April 1991, mid-term, following the resignation of Bill Van der Zalm. She resigned when the Party was defeated at the polls at the next election.

. . . .

Then prime minister, Brian Mulroney appointed Judith Parrish as a Citizenship judge. She was the former wife of M.P. and Cabinet Minister Paul Dick. When accused of breaching conflict of interest guidelines, Mr. Mulroney said that he was "advancing the cause of women" when he made the patronage appointment. Parrish had been receiving $3,200 per month in spousal support from Dick. Don Boudria, a Liberal M.P., noted that Parrish's appointment to the well-paid position would allow Dick to end those payments (*The [Ottawa] Citizen* [25 March 1993], A3).

. . . .

Kim Campbell became the first woman to become prime minister. She resigned on November 4, 1993, after only 133 days in office, following the defeat of the Progressive Conservatives. Her Party retained only 2 seats in the election.

The number of women elected at the federal level increased in the October 1993 election to 18 per cent, compared to 13.5 per cent in 1988. Of the total 23 Cabinet minister positions, only 4 are women. The Senate had only 16 women out of a total of 103 Senators. Provincially, no region has elected more than 25.3 per cent women members of the Legislature ("Work in Progress," CACSW [1994], at 29, 107).

. . . .

Maryka Omatsu became the first woman of Japanese ancestry to be appointed as judge of the Ontario Provincial Court. She was the first East Asian woman judge in Canada. She is known among her colleagues as "the serene judge." She has said that this is a sobriquet which she probably earned because "I am so even keeled. I don't get impatient or angry." On her work and the work of other visible minority female judges, she is quoted as remarking, "If we're duds, people will say 'I told you so.' If we do our jobs well, people will disregard our visibility" ("Profiles," [May 1994], vol. 4, no. 2).

. . . .

On July 29, the Canadian Panel on Violence Against Women released its report, *Changing the Landscape: Ending Violence, Achieving Equality*. It was the world's first comprehensive national study of violence against women. The Report contained a National Action Plan with almost 500 recommendations. Status of Women Canada is coordinating the federal government's response to the Report. A four-member Aboriginal Circle was part of the Panel. Thirty-eight of the Panel's recommendations were specific to the situations of Aboriginal and Inuit women (Status of Women Canada, [1993], 6 *Perspectives*, 3).

On December 1, the United Nations General Assembly adopted the Canadian-initiated "Declaration on the Elimination of Violence Against Women." This Declaration calls on governments to prevent and punish acts of violence, "whether perpetrated by the state, within the general community, or within the home" (Status of Women Canada, *Perspectives*).

1994

Delia Opekokew, a Cree woman who was the first Aboriginal woman to be admitted to the Bars of Ontario (1979) and Saskatchewan (1983), became the first woman to run for leadership of the Assembly of First Nations. Her platform focussed on issues at the reserve level rather than on constitutional problems.

. . . .

Judy Tyabji, an M.L.A. in the British Columbia legislature, was told by Mr. Justice John Spencer of the B.C. Supreme Court that her "attention as a custodial parent would be, to a degree, sidetracked by her career agenda" and he denied her custody of her children. Her former spouse also worked full-time but the judge said that in his view the children would benefit "more from their father's low-key approach to life than from the mother's wider-ranging ambition."

. . . .

Jocelyne Bourgon was the first woman to be appointed as Clerk of the Privy Council (*The [Toronto] Globe and Mail* [25 February 1994], A1).

. . . .

Monica Goulet became the first Aboriginal woman to become President of the Canadian Research Institute for the Advancement of Women (CRIAW). She is a Metis woman of Cree, Saulteaux and French ancestry.

. . . .

Rose Boyko, a T'Sekani woman from B.C., became the first Aboriginal woman appointed by the federal government to a superior court, when she was appointed to the Ontario High Court (General Division) in Newmarket, Ontario. She received her law degree in 1980 and was a legal advisor in the Department of Justice from 1982–91, in Ottawa, Edmonton, and Saskatoon. At the time of her appointment to the bench, she was director of the Indian Taxation Secretariat.

. . . .

In March, the panel of judges sitting on the B.C. Court of Appeal was comprised of three women justices — for the first time in the 88-year history of the Court.

. . . .

In May 1994, the Federal Court of Canada ruled, in a case brought by Susan Thidaudeau, that the *Income Tax Act* was discriminatory and unconstitutional in that it required single parents to pay taxes on child support payments received from the non-custodial parent. This requirement was held to fall disproportionately on women. The case has been appealed to the Supreme Court of Canada.

3. Women in Canada in the 1990s: Comparative Statistical Analyses

In this section, a range of statistical material is profiled and compared in order to situate women in contemporary Canadian society. The range of women's experiences and their relations to economic and social indicators provides a basis for identifying and debating current and ongoing issues, strategy and action.

Materials of the sections are extracted from the following sources:

Human Rights Directorate, Department of Secretary of State, Convention on the Elimination of All Forms of Discrimination Against Women, *Third Report of Canada*, 1992 (covering the period January 1, 1987, to December 31, 1990). Catalogue No. Ci51-76/1992E. Excerpts from pp. 2–21; 29–36. Source of information from Canadian Heritage. Reproduced with the permission of the Minister of Supply and Services Canada, 1994.

Canadian Advisory Council on the Status of Women, "Work in Progress: Tracking Women's Equality in Canada," June 1994. Excerpts. Reprinted by permission of Canadian Advisory Council on the Status of Women, Ottawa, Ontario.

Punam Khosla, "Review of the Situation of Women in Canada," July 1993. Reprinted by permission of National Action Committee on the Status of Women, Toronto, Ontario.

Donna S. Lero and Karen L. Johnson, *110 Canadian Statistics on Work & Family*, April 1994. Excerpts. Reprinted by permission of Canadian Advisory Council on the Status of Women, Ottawa, Ontario.

Status of Women Canada, "Perspectives," vol. 6, no. 3, fall 1993. Source of information from Status of Women Canada *Perspectives*. Reprinted by permission of Communication Unit, Status of Women Canada, Ottawa, Ontario.

Statistics Canada, *The Daily* (18 November 1993; 2 March 1993). Reproduced by authority of the Minister of Industry, 1994.

Nancy Zukewich Ghalam, *Women in the Workplace*, 2d ed. (Ottawa: Statistics Canada, March 1993). Reproduced by authority of the Minister of Industry, 1994.

The Globe & Mail (5 April 1994), A8. Reprinted by permission of The Globe & Mail.

Chantal Maille, "Primed for Power: Women in Canadian Politics," Canadian Advisory Council on the Status of Women, November 1990. Reprinted by permission of Canadian Advisory Council on the Status of Women, Ottawa, Ontario.

Crossing the Bar: A Century of Women's Experience "Upon the Rough and Troubled Seas of Legal Practices" in Ontario, 1993. Reprinted by permission of The Law Society of Upper Canada Archives, Toronto, Ontario.

Parallel Report to C.E.D.A.W., *Second Report of Canada*, 1990. Reprinted by permission of National Action Committee on the Status of Women, Toronto, Ontario.

Convention on the Elimination of All Forms of Discrimination Against Women, Third Report of Canada, 1992

Canadian Advisory Council on the Status of Women, "Work in Progress: Tracking Women's Equality in Canada," June 1994

Other Sources

4. The guidelines issued by the Committee on the Elimination of Discrimination against Women request States Parties to submit data that reflect the actual realities and general conditions that exist in the country.... The present statistical overview and the figures and tables that accompany it are also provided to meet the Committee's request....

I. SOCIAL CHARACTERISTICS

5. Women continue to constitute a slight majority of the Canadian population. In 1990, 50.7 per cent of all Canadians were female.

6. Women's representation is especially high in older age groups. In 1990, women accounted for 55.3 per cent of all 65–74-year-olds, 60.5 per cent of those aged 75–84, and 69.9 per cent of people over the age of 85.

[6.] Women in Canada have an average life expectancy of 80 years and are often assumed to have excellent health, with access to a public-funded health-care system...but quantity (length) of life is not a measure of quality. Moreover, wide disparities exist amongst women.

The poverty rate for women aged 65 and older in 1991 is 25 per cent.

The poverty rate for unattached women aged 65 and older is 47.4 per cent.

Canada's system of social support — which is currently under review — includes universal medicare, Old Age Security (OAS), the Guaranteed Income Supplement (GIS), and the Canada Assistance Program (CAP). Women rely heavily on these programs. Cuts made since 1985 have eroded the social safety net and could have serious consequences for many women.

[6.] While 85 per cent of older men receive pension benefits, the figure for women is less than 50 per cent (Punam Khosla, "Review of the Situation of Women in Canada," National Action Committee on the Status of Women, July 1993, p. 28).

Continued

Convention on the Elimination of All Forms of Discrimination Against Women, Third Report of Canada, 1992

Canadian Advisory Council on the Status of Women, "Work in Progress: Tracking Women's Equality in Canada," June 1994

Other Sources

8. Substantial proportions of women in Canada are immigrants and members of visible minority groups. In 1986, immigrants made up close to 16 per cent of the female population. Just over 6 per cent of women were identified as members of visible minorities, while close to 3 per cent had aboriginal origins.

10. The number of female-headed lone-parent families is growing. By 1986, 701,900 families were headed by a female lone parent, a 19 per cent increase since 1981. These families represented 10.4 per cent of all families in 1986, compared with 9.3 per cent in 1981.

11. ...Between 1981 and 1986, the number of women living in one-person households increased 15 per cent....

12. Elderly women are, by far, the group most likely to live alone. In 1986, 38 per cent of all women over age 65 lived alone. This compared with just 15 per cent of elderly men.

18. The incidence of divorce rose somewhat during the 1980s. Between 1981 and 1988, the number of divorces per 100,000 married women increased 11 per cent....

19. Women retain custody of the majority of children involved in divorces. In 1988, wives were granted custody of 76 per cent of all children involved in divorces; in cases where the wife was the applicant, this proportion was 83 per cent. As well, in another 10 per cent of cases, joint custody was awarded.

21. Canadian women are having fewer children. The general fertility rate, that is, the number of births per

[12.] In 1990, women aged 55 and over living alone made up 29 per cent of all subsidized households.

[19.] For the years 1982–86, the percentage of women impoverished by separation or divorce was 35 per cent; the percentage of men impoverished was 9 per cent.

For the same period, the average family income for women was 57 per cent of pre-divorce level; for men, 82 per cent.

[10.] Data from the 1991 Census indicate that 82 per cent of lone-parent families (with unmarried children of any age) were headed by women. The proportion is higher when only families with children under age 13 are considered. In 1988, fully 92 per cent of lone-parent families with children in this age range were headed by women.

Female lone parents are less likely than other parents to be employed. In 1991, 52 per cent of female lone parents with children under age 16 were employed, down from 54 per cent in 1981.

Almost 62 per cent of female lone-parent families lived below the low income cut-off in 1991, up from 60.6 per cent in 1990. (Donna S. Lero and Karen L. Johnson, *110 Canadian Statistics on Work & Family*, The Canadian Advisory Council on the Status of Women, April 1994, pp. 14–15).

Continued

Convention on the Elimination of All Forms of Discrimination Against Women, Third Report of Canada, 1992

1,000 women aged 15–49, fell from 56.7 in 1981 to 54.1 in 1988.

28. Disabilities are slightly more common among women than among men. In 1986, 14 per cent of women were disabled, compared with 13 per cent of men.

29. This overall difference was entirely attributable to a relatively high rate of disability among elderly women. In 1986, 57 per cent of women aged 75–84 were disabled, compared with 48 per cent of men in this age range....

30. Female disability rates, though, were slightly lower than those of men for all age groups younger than 75.

31. Elderly women with disabilities are also more likely than their male counterparts to live in institutions. In 1986, 19 per cent of disabled women aged 65 and over resided in institutions, compared with 12 per cent of men.... These variations in living arrangements occur because elderly women are more likely than elderly men to be widowed, and therefore, do not have a spouse to care for them at home.

32. As of November 1990, 6 per cent of all AIDS cases (fewer than 260) involved women....

44. ...a higher proportion of female than male homicide victims are killed by an immediate relative. In 1988, 57 per cent of all female homicide victims were killed by a family member, whereas the figure for men was 24 per cent.

Canadian Advisory Council on the Status of Women, "Work in Progress: Tracking Women's Equality in Canada," June 1994

[28.–30.] In 1991, the disability rate for women was 16.2 per cent while the disability rate for men was 14.8 per cent.

In 1991, 48.4 per cent of women aged 65 and over were disabled.

The percentage of ever-married women with disabilities who have been sexually or physically assaulted by their male partner was 39 per cent while the percentage for the overall female population was 29 per cent.

The percentage of women with disabilities aged 15–64 whose highest level of schooling is a university degree was 5.6 per cent compared with 12.2 per cent of women without disabilities who have a university degree.

[31.] In 1991, 17.3 per cent of disabled women aged 65 and over were residing in institutions while 10.7 per cent of men were in institutions.

[44.] In 1991, the relationship of women violent-crime victims to the accused were:

spouse or ex-spouse	43%
other family member	7%
friend/business relation	13%
acquaintance	16%

Other Sources

[28.–31.] Roughly 16 per cent of a sample of 7,000 Canadian employees surveyed by the Conference Board of Canada reported that they or other members of their households provided care to an elderly, disabled, or infirm family member. Women were much more likely than men to report primary responsibility in their families for the care of these relatives: 60 per cent of women reported that they were primarily responsible for the care of dependent relatives (including their spouse's parents and other extended family), compared with 26 per cent of men (Donna S. Lero and Karen L. Johnson, *110 Canadian Statistics on Work & Family*, The Canadian Advisory Council on the Status of Women, April 1994, p. 20).

[44.] On July 29, 1993, the Canadian Panel on Violence Against Women released its report, "Changing the Landscape: Ending Violence — Achieving Equality." It is the world's first comprehensive national study of violence against women. The goals of the Panel are to eliminate violence

Continued

Convention on the Elimination of All Forms of Discrimination Against Women, Third Report of Canada, 1992

Canadian Advisory Council on the Status of Women, "Work in Progress: Tracking Women's Equality in Canada," June 1994

Other Sources

against women and achieve women's equality. The report contains a National Action Plan of almost 500 recommendations. Status of Women Canada is coordinating the federal response to the Panel's report. A four-member Aboriginal Circle was part of the Canadian Panel on Violence Against Women. 38 of the recommendations were specific to the situations of Aboriginal and Inuit women (Status of Women Canada, "Perspectives", vol. 6, no. 3, fall 1993, p. 1).

On November 18, 1993, Statistics Canada released results from the "Violence Against Women Survey": One-half (51%) of Canadian women have experienced at least one incident of physical or sexual violence since the age of 16. Twenty-five per cent of all women have experienced physical or sexual violence at the hands of a current or past marital partner since the age of 16. One-fifth (19%) of women who experienced violence by a previous partner reported that the violence occurred following or during separation and, in one-third of these cases, the violence increased in severity at the time of separation.

One in five violent incidents reported to this survey were serious enough to result in physical injury. A higher proportion of wife assault incidents (45%) resulted in injury than did other sexual or physical assaults.

Almost one-half (45%) of all women experienced violence by men known to them (dates, boyfriends, marital partners, friends, family, neighbours, etc.), while 23 per cent of women experienced violence by a stranger....

Almost 60 per cent of women who experienced a sexual assault were the targets of more than one such incident.

Continued

Convention on the Elimination of All Forms of Discrimination Against Women, Third Report of Canada, 1992

Canadian Advisory Council on the Status of Women, "Work in Progress: Tracking Women's Equality in Canada," June 1994

Other Sources

Ten per cent of women experienced violence in the twelve months prior to the survey.

Experiences of violence were reported by women from all socio-economic backgrounds. However, the highest 12-month rates of violence were reported by women with household incomes under $15,000, by young women 18 to 24 years of age, and by those with some post-secondary education.

In all, 14 per cent of all violent incidents reported by respondents to this survey were reported to the police. Wife assault and other physical assaults (26% and 28%) were more likely than sexual assaults (6%) to be reported.

Thirty-three per cent of all incidents reported to the police resulted in a charge against a perpetrator.

...in only 9 per cent of violent incidents did victims report using the services of a social agency (Statistics Canada, *The Daily*, November 18, 1993).

On December 1, 1993, the United Nations General Assembly adopted the "Canadian-initiated" Declaration on the Elimination of Violence Against Women. The Declaration is the first UN document to contain an "extensive definition of forms of violence against women, including physical, sexual and psychological violence." The Declaration calls on governments to prevent and punish acts of violence, "whether perpetrated by the state, within the general community or within the home" (Status of Women Canada, "Perspectives").

The United Nations High Commission for Refugees (UNHCR) is to appoint (for a 3-year term) a special investigator into violence against women and called on governments around the world to end sex discrimination. The investigator is expected to

Continued

Convention on the Elimination of All Forms of Discrimination Against Women, Third Report of Canada, 1992	Canadian Advisory Council on the Status of Women, "Work in Progress: Tracking Women's Equality in Canada," June 1994	Other Sources

make annual reports to the UNHCR beginning in 1995 (*Globe and Mail*, April 5, 1994, A8).

45. As well, wives are more likely than husbands to be murdered by their spouse. In 1988, 70 women were killed by their husbands, compared with 21 men who were killed by their wives. Nonetheless, the number of women murdered by their spouse in 1988 was one of the lowest totals in the last decade.

[45.] The percentage of women homicide victims killed by male partners during the period 1981–90 was 48 per cent. For the period 1974–92, the ratio of husband victims to wife victims was 1:3.2.

52. Women are less likely than men to be victims of violent crime. In 1987, there were 77 violent criminal incidents per 1,000 women aged 15 and over, compared with 90 incidents per 1,000 adult men.

[52.] In 1991, women's share of violent crime victims was 49 per cent.

39 per cent of women have been sexually assaulted. 51 per cent of women have experienced physical or sexual violence. 29 per cent of women have been assaulted by their spouses.

In 1993, the percentage of women who do not report violent incidents:

sexual assault	93%
physical assault	71%
wife assault	73%

53. Separated and divorced women are especially vulnerable to violent attack. In 1987, there were 265 violent crimes for every 1,000 separated or divorced women, the highest rate for any marital group, male or female.

II. EDUCATION

55. While the level of educational attainment of Canadians increased during the 1980s, women are still somewhat less likely than men to be university graduates. By 1989, 10 per cent of women aged 15 and over had earned a degree, up from 7 per cent in 1981. Degree-holders accounted for 14 per cent of adult men in 1989, compared with 11 per cent in 1981.

Continued

Convention on the Elimination of All Forms of Discrimination Against Women, Third Report of Canada, 1992

Canadian Advisory Council on the Status of Women, "Work in Progress: Tracking Women's Equality in Canada," June 1994

Other Sources

56. A higher proportion of women than men have earned certificates or diplomas from postsecondary institutions such as community colleges. In 1989, 15 per cent of women were graduates from these institutions, compared with 12 per cent of men....

57. The increase in the proportion of women with university degrees reflects the fact that women now make up the majority of undergraduate students. In 1989–90, 52 per cent of all full-time undergraduates were women, up from 47 per cent in 1981–82.... From 1981–82 to 1989–90, female undergraduate enrolment rose 42 per cent, compared with a 15 per cent rise in the number of male undergraduates.

58. Women's representation in graduate programs also increased sharply, although they remain a minority of full-time graduate students. Between 1981–82 and 1989–90, the number of female graduate students rose 45 per cent, compared with a 22 per cent increase for men. By 1989–90, women accounted for 41 per cent of all graduate students, up from 37 per cent in 1981–82.

59. The majority of part-time university students are women...by 1989–90, women made up 64 per cent of part-time undergraduates, compared with 60 per cent in 1981–82. As well, at the graduate level, 51 per cent of part-time students were women in 1989–90, up from 41 per cent in 1981–82.

60. At both the undergraduate and graduate levels, women are more likely than men to enrol in programs such as education, the humanities, and social sciences. By contrast, they are

[57.] Women's share of undergraduate diplomas in 1991 was 57.7 per cent.

[58.] Women's share of graduate diplomas in 1991 was 46 per cent.

[57.] During the 1950s, only 4 per cent of those enrolled in Ontario law schools were women. By the 1980s, women comprised 50 per cent of law school students (*Crossing the Bar: A Century of Women's Experience-"Upon the Rough and Troubled Seas of Legal Practice" in Ontario*, The Law Society of Upper Canada Archives, Toronto, 1993, p. 26).

[59.] Tuition fees for postsecondary programs rose by an average of 40 to 80 per cent between 1985–86 and 1991–92, and climbed a further 10–20 per cent for the 1992–93 academic year. The burden of these fees explains the high percentage of women who are part-time students. In 1990–91, 32 per cent of all part-time, mature women students were clerical workers (Punam Khosla, "Review of the Situation of Women in Canada," National Action Committee on the Status of Women, July 1993, p. 22).

Continued

Convention on the Elimination of All Forms of Discrimination Against Women, Third Report of Canada, 1992

Canadian Advisory Council on the Status of Women, "Work in Progress: Tracking Women's Equality in Canada," June 1994

Other Sources

generally less likely than men to be in fields such as engineering, the physical sciences, mathematics, architecture, economics, and computer science.

61. Throughout the 1980s, women outnumbered men in community colleges. Women accounted for 55 per cent of full-time community college students in 1988–89, up from 53 per cent in 1981–82.

62. Women attending community colleges are much more likely than men to enrol in health sciences (particularly nursing) and in social and educational services programs, while their representation in engineering and applied sciences, natural sciences, and primary industry programs is relatively low.

64. Women in older age groups and women born outside Canada are the most likely to have literacy problems. In 1989, 36 per cent of women aged 55–69 had limited reading skills, compared with 15 per cent of women aged 35–54 and 6 per cent of those aged 16–24. At the same time, 32 per cent of immigrant women had limited reading abilities in English and French, whereas this was the case for only 11 per cent of women born in Canada. Again, these distributions are similar to those for men.

65. In 1988, close to half (46 per cent) of all women reported that they knew how to use a computer. This was slightly lower than the proportion of men (48 per cent).

66. The tasks for which women and men use computers, however, differ. Women are slightly more likely than men to do word processing and data entry, whereas men are

[64.] Eighty per cent of federal language training money goes to Language Instruction for Newcomers to Canada which does not provide any training allowances, thereby cutting off immigrant women many of whom work a double day to survive. The program is also not open to refugee claimants and Canadian citizens. This eliminates the training option for non-anglo women...who previously worked in factories where they could operate in their native language, and who are now laid off. They are now blocked from gaining the language skills they need to find other work (Punam Khosla, "Review of the Situation of Women in Canada," National Action Committee on the Status of Women, July 1993, p. 21).

Continued

Convention on the Elimination of All Forms of Discrimination Against Women, Third Report of Canada, 1992

Canadian Advisory Council on the Status of Women, "Work in Progress: Tracking Women's Equality in Canada," June 1994

Other Sources

more likely to analyze data and do programming.

III. ECONOMIC CHARACTERISTICS

67.   The proportion of women in the labour force continues to rise. In 1989, 58 per cent of women were in the labour force, up from 52 per cent in 1981...women made up 44 per cent of the total labour force in 1989, compared with 41 per cent in 1981.

68.   Increases in labour force participation have been particularly pronounced among women aged 25–54. From 1981 to 1989, the percentage of 25–44-year-old women in the labour force rose from 65 per cent to 77 per cent, while the figure for those aged 45–54 went from 56 per cent to 68 per cent. Despite these increases, participation rates of women in these age ranges remain well below those of their male contemporaries, more than 90 per cent of whom were in the labour force in 1989.

70.   Labour force participation rates of women with children have also increased sharply. In 1989, for example, 62 per cent of women with pre-school-aged children were in the labour force, compared with 47 per cent in 1981. Over the same period, the participation rate of mothers with school-aged children rose from 61 per cent to 75 per cent.

71.   The rise in labour force participation by mothers has been accompanied by increasing demands for child care. In 1990, there were 321,000 licensed day care centre spaces and family day care spaces. This was almost three times the amount available in 1980 (109,000). Even so, just 18 per

[67.]   In 1991, women's share of the total work force was 45.3 per cent.

[67.]   In 1991, the labour force participation rate of women had reached 60.9 per cent (Statistics Canada, *The Daily*, Tuesday, 2 March 1993, p. 2).

[68.]   Much of the gains made by women since the sixties are in serious danger of being eroded. This was evident in the reversal of the long-term trend of women entering the workforce in increasing numbers each year. For the first time in more than twenty-five years, women's workforce participation rates dropped in both 1991 and 1992 and the decline is continuing into 1993 (Punam Khosla, "Review of the Situation of Women in Canada," National Action Committee on the Status of Women, July 1993, p. 3).

[70.]   In 1991, the labour force participation rate for women with all children less than 6 years was 67.2 per cent (Statistics Canada, *The Daily*, Tuesday, 2 March 1993, p. 4).

[71.]   Under the provisions of the Canada Assistance Plan, provinces and territories may cost-share certain elements of government expenditures related to child-care services (in particular, fee subsidies to lower-income families).... Information collected for the Special Parliamentary

Continued

| **Convention on the Elimination of All Forms of Discrimination Against Women, Third Report of Canada, 1992** | **Canadian Advisory Council on the Status of Women, "Work in Progress: Tracking Women's Equality in Canada," June 1994** | **Other Sources** |

cent of pre-school-age children with mothers working outside the home were in licensed day care spaces. The vast majority of children in need of day care were looked after either by baby-sitters or relatives.

Committee on Child Care indicated that only 15 per cent of those families who were eligible for either a full or partial subsidy in 1987 actually received assistance. In 1990, the federal government capped the contributions it would provide in cost-sharing under the Canada Assistance Plan to Ontario, Alberta, and British Columbia. Since then, the pressures of increased welfare costs ... and further reductions in federal transfer payments have constrained funds that might have been utilized to expand and support the development of licensed child-care facilities, and have further jeopardized the availability of subsidized spaces for children in low-income and single-parent families.

Other countries have been more willing to develop and support national child-care programs, particularly when the provision of high-quality care is viewed either as an essential service to support employment and economic growth, or as a critical component in young children's education and development (Donna S. Lero and Karen L. Johnson, *110 Canadian Statistics on Work & Family*, The Canadian Advisory Council on the Status of Women, April 1994, p. 32).

72. Women still bear the primary burden of family and home care, even when they are employed outside the home. In 1986, working women averaged 3.1 hours a day on domestic and child care duties. This was more than double the 1.5 hours that employed men devoted to such activities. Women who identified their primary activity as keeping house spent 6.0 hours per day on these tasks.

73. Part of the increase in women's labour force participation reflects shifts in the distribution of employ-

[72.] In 1992, women spent 4.5 hours per day doing unpaid work while men averaged 2.6 hours.

In 1990, women lost an average 5.2 days of paid work per year due to personal or family responsibilities while men lost only 0.9 days.

[72.] In dual-earner couples in which both parents were employed full-time, the majority of wives (52%) retained all of the responsibility for daily housework, while 28 per cent had most of the responsibility. Equal sharing of housework was reported in 10 per cent of these families, and in the remaining 10 per cent, the husband had all or most of the responsibility (1990 data) (Donna S. Lero and Karen L. Johnson, *110 Canadian Statistics on Work & Family*, The Canadian Advisory Council on the Status of Women, April 1994, p. 8).

Continued

Convention on the Elimination of All Forms of Discrimination Against Women, Third Report of Canada, 1992

Canadian Advisory Council on the Status of Women, "Work in Progress: Tracking Women's Equality in Canada," June 1994

Other Sources

ment from goods-producing to service industries. During the 1980s, almost all growth in the economy occurred in the service sector, where women constitute the majority of workers. In fact, the increase in the number of women in the service sector accounted for two-thirds of all labour force growth between 1981 and 1989.

74. In 1989, 53 per cent of service sector workers were women, up from 50 per cent in 1981. Overall, 83 per cent of working women were employed in the service sector, compared with 58 per cent of male labour force participants.

76. ...a large majority of female workers are still concentrated in occupations in which women have traditionally been employed. In 1989, 72 per cent of employed women worked in clerical jobs, service positions, sales, nursing and related health occupations, or teaching....

77. Clerical jobs constitute, by far, the largest single occupational category for women. In 1989, 31 per cent of all working women were in clerical positions...over 80 per cent of clerical workers were women, a slight increase over 79 per cent in 1982.

78. There are also relatively large shares of women in service jobs, sales, nursing and related health occupations, and teaching. In 1989, 17 per cent of female workers were in service positions; 10 per cent were in sales; 9 per cent were in nursing; and 6 per cent were teachers. This distribution is similar to the pattern in the early 1980s. As with clerical occupations, these fields have relatively large female components. In 1989, women

In 1991, 11 per cent of women in two-parent families with at least one child under age 6 and 6 per cent of comparable lone mothers missed time from work each week because of personal or family responsibilities.... All of these figures were higher than those for comparable fathers. In fact, the presence of young children had little effect on the work absences of fathers in two-parents families: 2 per cent of these men with pre-school-aged children lost time from work, versus 1 per cent of those whose youngest child was aged 6–15 (Nancy Zukewich Ghalam, *Women in the Workplace*, 2d ed. [Ottawa: Statistics Canada, March 1993], p. 17).

[76.–77.] In 1991, the three largest occupation categories for women were Clerical, Service, and Managerial and Administrative. Together, they accounted for 58 per cent of the experienced female labour force. For women, Clerical Occupations and Service Occupations ranked 1st and 2nd in all provinces and territories. The three largest occupation groups for men remained unchanged from 1986 — Managerial and Administrative, Construction, and Service Occupations. Together, these groups accounted for 35 per cent of the experienced male labour force. In general, male workers were more dispersed among the occupational groups than were female workers (Statistics Canada, *The Daily*, Tuesday, 2 March 1993, p. 10).

Continued

| **Convention on the Elimination of All Forms of Discrimination Against Women, Third Report of Canada, 1992** | **Canadian Advisory Council on the Status of Women, "Work in Progress: Tracking Women's Equality in Canada," June 1994** | **Other Sources** |

made up 85 per cent of people employed in nursing and related health occupations, 66 per cent of teachers, 57 per cent of service personnel, and 46 per cent of salespeople. These proportions were all above 1982 levels.

79. During the last decade, women's employment in managerial and administrative positions grew dramatically. Between 1982 and 1989, the number of female managers and administrators more than doubled.[1] Because of this increase, in 1989, the managerial and administrative category was the third largest occupational group for women, accounting for 11 per cent of all female workers...

[79.] The number of workers in the Managerial/Administrative Occupation category (e.g. accountants, human resource managers, and sales and advertising managers) grew faster than the number in any other broad occupation category, increasing by 30 per cent from 1986 to 1991. The number of women increased much faster than the number of men — 55 per cent versus 18 per cent (Statistics Canada, *The Daily*, Tuesday, 2 March 1993, p. 8).

[79.] While women's professional and managerial employment seems to have grown dramatically — by 10.25 per cent over the last three years and 27 per cent between 1981 and 1991, a substantial portion of this is due to job reclassification and changes in occupational definitions. For example, women who were previously classified as retail workers are now called managers of small two person retail areas in department stores despite little or no change in their wages or working conditions. Also, as women move into key occupations such as pharmacy and law, their work status and wages are far lower than their male counterparts (Punam Khosla, "Review of the Situation of Women in Canada," National Action Committee on the Status of Women, July 1993, p. 13).

---

[1] Changes in the managerial and administrative group should be interpreted with caution. Refinement of the occupational classification by the Labour Force Survey in 1984 had a pronounced effect on employment figures in this category. As much as 40 per cent of the increase in the proportion of women in this group may be attributable to new occupational definitions. But even without this artificial boost, there was still considerable growth in women's employment in this category.

Continued

Convention on the Elimination of All Forms of Discrimination Against Women, Third Report of Canada, 1992

Canadian Advisory Council on the Status of Women, "Work in Progress: Tracking Women's Equality in Canada," June 1994

Other Sources

80. Women's participation in several other professional occupations also increased. For example, between 1982 and 1989, the number of women in social science professions, excluding university teaching, rose 52 per cent. In fact, women made up 57 per cent of all people in these fields in 1989 whereas the 1982 figure had been 48 per cent. In the same period, the number of women employed as health professionals such as doctors more than doubled, so that by 1989, 33 per cent of people in these professions were women, compared with 18 per cent in 1982. On the other hand, women still accounted for only 19 per cent of those in natural sciences, engineering, and mathematics in 1989 although this was up from 15 per cent in 1982.

[80.] In 1972, women comprised only 3 per cent of the legal profession in Ontario. In 1991, 20 per cent of practising lawyers were women (*Crossing the Bar: A Century of Women's Experience "Upon the Rough and Troubled Seas of Legal Practice" in Ontario*, The Law Society of Upper Canada Archives, Toronto, 1993, p. 27).

[80.] Between 1986 and 1991, the number of women economists increased by 65 per cent, social workers by 49 per cent, lawyers and notaries by 71 per cent, educational and vocational counsellors by 59 per cent, and accountants and auditors by 42 per cent. Women also showed a large percentage increase for judges and magistrates (82%), although their numbers remained small. Among architects, engineers and community planners, women more than doubled their numbers over the 1986–1991 period, although they continue to make up a small percentage of the total number.

In 1991, the four most frequent occupations for women were the same as in 1986: secretaries and stenographers, sales clerks, bookkeepers and accounting clerks, and cashiers and tellers. Combined, these four specific occupations represented 23 per cent of the experienced female labour force in 1991, down slightly from 25 per cent in 1986 (Statistics Canada, *The Daily*, Tuesday, 2 March 1993, p. 10).

Continued

Convention on the Elimination of All Forms of Discrimination Against Women, Third Report of Canada, 1992

Canadian Advisory Council on the Status of Women, "Work in Progress: Tracking Women's Equality in Canada," June 1994

Other Sources

81. Women continue to be significantly under-represented in what have traditionally been male-dominated blue-collar jobs. In 1989, women made up around 20 per cent of people employed in primary occupations and in manufacturing jobs such as processing, machining, and product fabricating. As well, there was little change in this pattern during the decade...by 1989, just 9 per cent of people in transportation and only 2 per cent of those in construction were women.

82. Women are less likely than men to be self-employed. In 1989, 9 per cent of all female workers, compared with 17 per cent of male workers, ran their own business.

83. Nonetheless, women's share of this sector has risen over the last decade. In 1989, 29 per cent of all self-employed people were women, up from 24 per cent in 1981. In fact, women accounted for almost half (45 per cent) of all growth in self-employment between 1985 and 1989.

86. Women are far more likely than men to work part-time. In 1989, 25 per cent of all employed women had part-time jobs, compared with just 8 per cent of men. The proportion of women working part-time, however, has fallen slightly since the mid-1980s. In 1985, for example, 26 per cent of employed women held part-time jobs.

87. Most women who work part-time do so by choice. In 1989, 39 per

[82.] Women make up the vast majority of unpaid family workers, that is, those whose unpaid work contributes directly to the operation of a farm, business, or professional practice owned or operated by a related household member. In 1991, eight out of ten unpaid family workers were women. Overall, however, this category accounted for just 1 per cent of total female employment (Nancy Zukewich Ghalam, *Women in the Workplace*, 2d ed. [Ottawa: Statistics Canada, 1993], p. 15).

[86.] In 1990, almost 30 per cent of all women worked mostly part-time, compared to only 12 per cent of all men. However, out of all women who worked in 1990, 45 per cent worked full-year, full-time, compared to 59 per cent for men (Statistics Canada, *The Daily*, Tuesday, 2 March, 1993, p. 5).

[86.] The percentage of all women working part-time increased slightly from 24.4 per cent in 1990 to 25.9 per cent in 1992 (Punam Khosla, "Review of the Situation of Women in Canada," National Action Committee on the Status of Women, July 1993, p. 7).

[87.] In 1991, the percentage of women working part-time because they

[87.] While 36 per cent of female part-time workers indicated a prefer-

Continued

Convention on the Elimination of All Forms of Discrimination Against Women, Third Report of Canada, 1992

cent reported they did not want full-time jobs; another 23 per cent were going to school; and 14 per cent cited personal or family responsibilities as the reason they worked part-time. Still, over 300,000 women, 22 per cent of those working part-time, did so because they could not find full-time employment.

93. Women are less likely than men to be union members. In 1988, 30 per cent of female workers, compared with 39 per cent of their male counterparts, were members of unions....

94. Women are generally less likely than men to be covered by either public or private pensions. Because eligibility for Canada or Quebec Pension Plans (CPP/QPP) is tied to employment, a smaller proportion of

Canadian Advisory Council on the Status of Women, "Work in Progress: Tracking Women's Equality in Canada," June 1994

could only find part-time work: 26.9 per cent.

Other Sources

ence for part-time employment in 1991, another 27 per cent were unable to find full-time positions. Other women worked part-time because they were going to school (22%) or because of personal or family responsibilities (13%) (Nancy Zukewich Ghalam, *Women in the Workplace*, 2d ed. [Ottawa: Statistics Canada, 1993], p. 5).

Whereas part-time work can reduce some of the pressures on employees with family responsibilities, the precarious nature of part-time work, the lack of access to benefits, and the growth in evening and weekend shift work can complicate efforts to harmonize paid work and dependant care; these factors also can threaten economic security (Donna S. Lero and Karen L. Johnson, *110 Canadian Statistics on Work & Family*, The Canadian Advisory Council on the Status of Women, April 1994, p. 1).

Between 1976 and 1991, women have consistently represented at least 70 per cent of total part-time employment (less than 30 hours per week) (Donna S. Lero and Karen L. Johnson, *110 Canadian Statistics on Work & Family*, The Canadian Advisory Council on the Status of Women, April 1994, p. 4).

[93.] ...only 6 per cent of workers of colour and aboriginal workers are in unions (Punam Khosla, "Review of the Situation of Women in Canada," National Action Committee on the Status of Women, July 1993, p. 17).

Continued

Convention on the Elimination of All Forms of Discrimination Against Women, Third Report of Canada, 1992

Canadian Advisory Council on the Status of Women, "Work in Progress: Tracking Women's Equality in Canada," June 1994

Other Sources

women than men participate in these programs. In the mid-1980s, for example, around 60 per cent of women aged 18–64, compared with more than 85 per cent of men, contributed to these plans. However, while the share of women in CPP/QPP programs has risen from around 55 per cent in the late 1970s, the figure for men has fallen from over 90 per cent.

95. Because CPP/QPP benefits depend on factors such as length of time worked and size of contributions, women receive fewer benefits than men. In 1986, the average CPP/QPP benefit paid to women was only about 60 per cent of that received by men.

[95.] The Canada/Quebec Pension Plan gap[2] was 58.8 per cent in 1993.

96. Women are less likely than men to participate in private pension plans. In 1988, 31 per cent of women in the labour force participated in such plans, compared with 42 per cent of men.

97. Women's lower participation in private pension plans is related to their concentration in both part-time work and in industries where pension coverage is less extensive than in industries where men predominate.

100. Women's share of total income has risen over the last decade and a half. In 1989, women's income accounted for 36 per cent of all income, up from 32 per cent in 1982 and 26 per cent in 1975.

101. Almost all the increase in women's share of total income occurred because more women are working. There has, in fact, been no reduction in the wage gap between

[101.] In 1991, the full-time full-year wage gap was 69.6 per cent. The wage gap calculated on all earnings (full and part-time) was 61.5 per cent.

[101.] While for men, youth is a period of deferred gratification for future earnings, women's low wages persist at all age levels. The false appearance of a relatively small wage

---

[2] The Canada/Quebec Pension Plan gap is the average monthly benefit for women as a percentage of that of men.

Continued

Convention on the Elimination of All Forms of Discrimination Against Women, Third Report of Canada, 1992

Canadian Advisory Council on the Status of Women, "Work in Progress: Tracking Women's Equality in Canada," June 1994

Other Sources

women and men since the mid-1980s. In 1988, the earnings of full-time female workers were 65 per cent those of men working full-time. While this figure was up from 60 per cent in 1975, it was actually slightly lower than that in 1984.

gap between young people artificially inflates the overall figures for women. Women between 35 and 44, who make up a quarter of the female workforce, are earning 58.9 per cent of the earnings of men in their age category and the gap grows further for older women who earn just 53.8 per cent of what older men make (Punam Khosla, "Review of the Situation of Women in Canada," National Action Committee on the Status of Women, July 1993, p. 9).

[101.] The wages of women of colour and aboriginal women who were working in full-time, full-year jobs are notably lower than those of other women, men of colour and other men. In 1985, Aboriginal women drew an average salary of 18,500 — very close to that of women of colour at $18,900. (See Table 3)

This, however is only one small part of the real picture. In 1989, a quarter of all aboriginal women had no income at all. In 1985, their unemployment rates were more than double those of Canadians overall at 22 per cent. Many women of colour work in low-paying 'underground' jobs and their wages are not recorded in official statistics.

Racial background clearly has an impact on wages, but more surprising is the relatively small gap between women by race compared to the larger gap in earnings by gender, showing that visible minority men, aboriginal men and white men all earn far more than any grouping of women (Punam Khosla, "Review of the Situation of Women in Canada," National Action Committee on the Status of Women, July 1993, p. 9).

102. The earnings gap between women and men is smaller for those

Continued

| **Convention on the Elimination of All Forms of Discrimination Against Women, Third Report of Canada, 1992** | **Canadian Advisory Council on the Status of Women, "Work in Progress: Tracking Women's Equality in Canada," June 1994** | **Other Sources** |

with higher levels of education. Still, in 1988, the average earnings of female university graduates working full-time all year were only 72 per cent those of comparable male graduates....

105.   Lone-parent families headed by women are among the most vulnerable to economic hardship. In 1989, 39 per cent of all female-headed lone-parent families had incomes below official low-income lines. While this was down from 48 per cent in 1985, the proportion of these families living on low incomes was still far greater than the figure for all husband-wife families with children (7 per cent).

106.   ...In 1989, 41 per cent of women aged 65 and over who lived alone had low incomes. This was a decline from 52 per cent in 1985 and 66 per cent in 1980.

109.   Although these data are not complete enough to permit in-depth analysis, they nevertheless show that significant progress has been made in many areas:

Representation of Women on Elected Public Bodies

House of Commons	1980 (5.0%)
	1985 (9.6%)
	1990 (13.6%)
Senate	1980 (10.2%)
	1985 (10.9%)
	1990 (13.5%)

Representation of Women in the Judiciary, 1990

| Federal Appointments (Superior Courts) | 8.7% |
| Provincial/Territorial Appointments (Lower Courts) | 9.0% |

[105.]   In 1990, the poverty rate for lone-parent families headed by women was 61 per cent. In 1991, this rate increased to 62 per cent. In 1993, the United Nations Committee on Economic, Social, and Cultural Rights criticized the Canadian government for failing to take action to eliminate poverty and improve the situation of single mothers.

[106.]   In 1991, 47.4 per cent of unattached women aged 65 and older had incomes below the low-income cut-offs.

[109.]   In 1993, 18 per cent of members of the Parliament of Canada were women.
In 1994, 15.5 per cent of Senators were women.
In 1994, there are 951 federally appointed judges. 123 of these are women (12.9 per cent). In the Supreme Court of Canada, 2 out of 9 are women; the Federal Court of Canada, 5 out of 35 are women; the Tax Court of Canada, 3 out of 25 are women; of the 10 federal Courts of Appeal, 23 out of 126 are women.
In 1993, the federal Cabinet had only 4 women out of a total of 23 Cabinet Ministers, and the Senate had only 16 women out of a total of 103 Senators. In provincial/territorial politics, women have made significant advances; however, no region has elected more than 25.3 per cent women Members of Parliament.

[109.]   Of total appointments to federal boards, agencies, commissions and Crown corporations as of 1990, women comprised 29 per cent of positions. The percentage of women appointed to management positions in the federal public service increased from 12 per cent in 1984 to 19.7 per cent in 1989 (Chantal Maillé, "Primed for Power: Women in Canadian Politics," Canadian Advisory Council on the Status of Women, November 1990, pp. 20–21).
The number of women appointed to positions as ambassadors, high commissioners, and consuls general increased from 2 to 17, and the number of women deputy ministers or equivalent level in the federal public service increased from 7 to 22. (Status of Women Canada, "Perspectives," vol. 6, no. 3 (fall 1993), p. 6).

Continued

| **Convention on the Elimination of All Forms of Discrimination Against Women, Third Report of Canada, 1992** | **Canadian Advisory Council on the Status of Women, "Work in Progress: Tracking Women's Equality in Canada," June 1994** | **Other Sources** |

Women in
Senior Government Positions

Cabinet Ministers	1985 (15.4%)
	1990 (18.4%)
Deputy and Associate Deputy Ministers	1985 (13.5%)
	1990 (18.9%)
Assistant Deputy Ministers or Equivalent	1985 (4.1%)
	1990 (10.4%)

IV. MEASURES ADOPTED BY THE GOVERNMENT OF CANADA

Protection of women's legal rights

141.   Through the Court Challenges Program, the Government provides financial support to groups and individuals to challenge laws perceived as contrary to the Canadian Constitution in light of, among other things, the guarantees of sexual equality (sections 15 and 28) of the *Canadian Charter of Rights and Freedoms*. In May 1990, the Court Challenges Program was renewed with $13.75 million over five years....

[141.]   In August 1993, then Prime Minister Kim Campbell announced the reinstatement of the Court Challenges Program, which had been abolished in February 1992. Prime Minister Jean Chrétien has committed his government to implementing a new version of the Court Challenges Program, which will be called the Charter Law Development Program and will be run by a non-profit agency operating at arm's length from government. Women are still waiting.

Legislative changes

142.   As discussed in the second report, the 1985 amendments to the *Indian Act* gave back Indian status to women who had lost it under previous discriminatory provisions of the Act. Women who had lost Indian status and band membership as a result of the provisions in the former section 12(1)(b) are entitled to regain status and membership upon application. First-generation descendants are also entitled to status and can apply to the bands for membership.

[142.]   Although the new law allows many women to have their Indian status reinstated, the effect of past discrimination persists through rules on how status is passed on to children. The new law has been characterized as racist, sexist, and in violation of women's cultural rights because it assumes that the unnamed fathers of Indian single mothers are non-Indian.

Bill C-31 also separates out Indian status and band membership. Band membership gives the right to live on

Continued

Convention on the Elimination of All Forms of Discrimination Against Women, Third Report of Canada, 1992	Canadian Advisory Council on the Status of Women, "Work in Progress: Tracking Women's Equality in Canada," June 1994	Other Sources

A comprehensive evaluation of the impacts of the legislation, conducted in consultation with national aboriginal organizations, was submitted to Parliament in December 1990. It stated that as a result of the amendments there has been a 19 per cent increase in the status Indian population in Canada. Women represent 58 per cent of all those who gained status and 77 per cent of those whose status was restored.

the band's reserve, and to have a share of income from band resources. Many reinstated women have not been accepted by their bands. Reasons vary, but shortage of resources is a crucial factor.

Canada's constitution guarantees equality for Aboriginal women and includes a commitment to the participation of Aboriginal representatives in constitutional changes that affect them. In 1992, the Federal Court of Appeal ruled that the federal government had violated the constitutional rights of Aboriginal women by excluding the Native Women's Association of Canada (NWAC) from the most recent round of constitutional talks.

National penal provisions

146. *Creating Choices*, the report of the Task Force on Federally Sentenced Women, a joint initiative of the Government and non-governmental organizations, including the Canadian Association of Elizabeth Fry Societies and aboriginal women's groups, was released in April 1990. In response, the Solicitor General of Canada announced on September 26, 1990 that the Prison for Women in Kingston will be replaced with five regional facilities, including a *Healing Lodge* for aboriginal inmates. This initiative, which will be implemented over a four-year period at a cost of approximately $50 million, will enable women to serve their sentences closer to their families and home communities.

[146.] In 1989, women made up less than 2 per cent of inmates in federal prisons and about 8 per cent of inmates in provincial/territorial custodial facilities. Aboriginal women were 14.4 per cent of women federal inmates and 29 per cent of women provincial/territorial inmates. Women prisoners are often confined far away from their families, and facilities for contact with their children are limited. Training programs are few, ill-prepare women for future jobs, and are determined by offence rather than need. In 1990, a joint government-NGO Task Force on Federally Sentenced Women recommended a number of reforms. Chief among these was replacing the Kingston prison with new regional prisons so that women would be closer to their families. Many of these recommendations have been accepted but not yet implemented.

Measures to ensure the advancement of women

147. In September 1988, the Minister Responsible for the Status of Women established a working group to develop a Plan of Action for Aboriginal Women and Economic Devel-

Continued

Convention on the Elimination of All Forms of Discrimination Against Women, Third Report of Canada, 1992

Canadian Advisory Council on the Status of Women, "Work in Progress: Tracking Women's Equality in Canada," June 1994

Other Sources

opment. The working groups consisted of the three national aboriginal women's organizations (the Native Women's Association of Canada, the Pauktiutit Inuit Women's Association of Canada and the Indian and Inuit Nurses of Canada) and Status of Women Canada.

148. The Plan of Action, now completed, provides recommendations in areas such as data collection for use in program and policy development, the facilitation of education and training, and mechanisms to increase aboriginal women's awareness of and access to economic development programs. The Plan is part of the Canadian Aboriginal Economic Development Strategy, Announced in June 1989, a key goal of which is to provide long-term employment and business opportunities to Canada's aboriginal citizens. A co-ordinator has been hired with the mandate to establish and implement the Plan.

[148.] In 1990, 60 per cent of Aboriginal women had total incomes under $10,000 per year. The labour force participation rate for Aboriginal women was 49.7 per cent in 1991. Aboriginal women face the same occupational segregation as non-Aboriginal women, but make less money and suffer higher unemployment. Aboriginal women are among the most disadvantaged groups in Canada. In 1990, the unemployment rate for Aboriginal women was 21.6 per cent, compared to 10.8 per cent for all women. While 83.3 per cent of Aboriginal women report their highest level of education to be at least secondary school, only 2.9 per cent had a university degree.

In 1986, 14.8 per cent of Aboriginal women aged 15 and over were lone parents, compared to 7 per cent for all Canadian women.

Governments in Canada have conducted several inquiries into the treatment of Aboriginal persons by the justice system, and a Royal Commission investigation on Canada's Aboriginal peoples is underway. However, it is patently clear that significant real progress is necessary in Canada to achieve FLS and CEDAW commitments for Aboriginal women.

149. The *Employment* Equity Act, described in paragraph 88 of Canada's second report, provides for comprehensive reviews of its provisions, operation and impact by a parliamentary committee. The first review will take

[149.] The CACSW's analysis of the first four years of this legislation demonstrates that women in the federally-regulated work force are still under-represented in the majority of occupations, that hirings and promo-

[149.] Little or no progress is being made for most women, particularly Aboriginal women, women of colour and disabled women. In some cases the position of women is actually worse. Without mandatory goals and

Continued

Convention on the Elimination of All Forms of Discrimination Against Women, Third Report of Canada, 1992

Canadian Advisory Council on the Status of Women, "Work in Progress: Tracking Women's Equality in Canada," June 1994

Other Sources

place in 1991, after the Act has been in force for five years. Subsequent reviews are to be held every three years. Consultations are presently taking place with employers, employer and labour organizations, designated group representatives, associations and government officials, on issues related to the *Employment Equity Act* in preparation for the parliamentary review.

tions actually accentuated this job segregation, and that part-time work is still largely women's work. Aboriginal women, racial minority women, and women with disabilities are still the most disadvantaged in terms of representation, job profile, salaries, and hirings and promotions.

timetables, women with disabilities, racial minority women and aboriginal women continue to be virtually excluded from the workforce, face discrimination both at entry and promotion and experience scandalous unemployment rates. The only group of women that are experiencing any advancement are white women, and it is at a glacial pace (Punam Khosla, "Review of the Situation of Women in Canada," National Action Committee on the Status of Women, July 1993, p. 23).

Prostitution

167. Bill C-149, *An Act to Amend the Criminal Code (Prostitution)*, came into force in December 1985 to respond to the nuisance created by street prostitution. Its main purpose was to make criminal three public activities when they are undertaken for the purpose of offering or purchasing sexual services: (a) stopping a motor vehicle; (b) impeding pedestrian or vehicular traffic; and (c) communicating for the purpose of prostitution in a public place...

168. In October 1990, after a three-year implementation period, the Standing Committee on Justice and the Solicitor General issued a report based on a parliamentary review of the soliciting provisions. The Committee' first recommendation called for the development of programs to provide funds to community-based agencies for prostitutes wishing to leave the street solicitation trade. The Committee also recommended that the *Identification of Criminals Act* be amended to allow for the fingerprinting and photographing of those charged under section 213 of the *Criminal Code*, whether as prostitutes or as customers. Finally, the Committee recommended that this section be amended to provide sentencing judges with the discretion to prohibit persons convicted of street

Continued

Convention on the Elimination of All Forms of Discrimination Against Women, Third Report of Canada, 1992

Canadian Advisory Council on the Status of Women, "Work in Progress: Tracking Women's Equality in Canada," June 1994

Other Sources

solicitation involving a motor vehicle from driving a motor vehicle for a period not to exceed three months, in addition to any other penalty imposed.

169. The Government will be submitting a response to the report in March 1991, after consultations with interested parties such as provincial and territorial governments, municipal governments and non-governmental organizations.

Women in politics and public life

171. As of November 6, 1990, 31.2 per cent of appointments to federal boards, agencies and commissions were women. As of October 1990, 15 out of 111 appointed senators were women. Between September 1984 and October 1990, the number of women serving at the deputy minister or equivalent level in the federal government tripled from 7 to 22.

Judiciary

172. In January 1987, there were 721 federally appointed judges holding active office, together with 82 supernumerary judges, for a total of 803. Of the total, 51 were women (6.3 per cent). As of January 1, 1991, there were 745 federally-appointed judges and 113 supernumerary judges, a total of 858. Of these, 84 were women (9.8 per cent).

Non-governmental organizations

181. Secretary of State's Women's Program is the primary federal source of financial and technical support to women's groups and other voluntary

[181.] Since 1988, the Women's Program, Secretary of State has had its budget reduced by more than 25 per cent. NAC's funding over the past five

Continued

| **Convention on the Elimination of All Forms of Discrimination Against Women, Third Report of Canada, 1992** | **Canadian Advisory Council on the Status of Women, "Work in Progress: Tracking Women's Equality in Canada," June 1994** | **Other Sources** |

organizations working to promote equality for women. The Program was renewed for five years, effective April 1, 1988, with priority to provide support for disadvantaged women such as disabled, immigrant and visible minority women, rural and isolated women, and native women.

years has been reduced from $700,000 to $270,000. CRIAW's funding was reduced by 45 per cent.

Disabled women

189. The Disabled Persons Secretariat has been continuously involved with the promotion of disabled women and with making this a priority issue. In 1988, the Secretariat held a forum dealing with research on disabled women in order to obtain knowledge on the specific obstacles that prevent disabled women from participating in Canada's social and economic activities to the same extent as other women. In 1989, the Secretariat funded the Dis-Abled Women's Network (DAWN) to carry out the research and publication of four documents that contribute to a better understanding of the specific barriers that disabled women must face in our society. Also, the Disabled Persons Participation Program provides direct funding for projects carried out by disabled women.

[189.] In 1992, the *National Transportation Act* included a commitment to ensure that transportation systems are accessible, but the pledge fell far short of the demands. Most cities have established alternative public transportation systems for people with disabilities, but these systems are usually over-subscribed, making spontaneous or unplanned trips difficult. For women with disabilities who live in rural or small urban settings, these services are non-existent.

The plight of disabled women is progressively gaining attention in Canada. The DisAbled Women's Network (DAWN) is identifying issues of importance. Governments have promoted self-reliance by funding disabled women's organizations, but the level of funding is inadequate.

[189] Funding Cuts to Dawn Canada

The national office of the Dis-Abled Women's Network (DAWN Canada) closed as of March 31, 1993 due to substantial cuts in the project funding received from the Secretary of State. The organization does not receive core funding to run their national office.

The funding cuts at the national level will not directly affect local chapters of DAWN, which are provincially funded, but these local chapters have now lost the centre of their network (Susan Briscoe, "DisAbled Women's Network: Cuts threaten dusk for DAWN," *Kinesis*, April 1993).

Case, Legislation, People and Subject Indices

CASE INDEX

LEGISLATION INDEX

PEOPLE INDEX

SUBJECT INDEX